THE GRAND DESIGN:
Joseph Ramée's Drawings for the Union College Campus

PAUL V. TURNER

APRIL 11 – MAY 26, 2013

Mandeville Gallery

Union College

Schenectady, New York

THE GRAND DESIGN:
Joseph Ramée's Drawings for Union College

PAUL V. TURNER

Fig. 1. Competition design for a Washington Monument, Baltimore. Perspective drawing, ink and watercolor, 49 x 72 cm., inscribed "J. Ramée, 1813."
COURTESY OF THE MARYLAND HISTORICAL SOCIETY

IN DECEMBER, 1932, a young Union College graduate, Codman Hislop, reported a remarkable discovery in the *Union Alumni Monthly*.[1] Hislop, later a professor of English at Union, explained that he had been looking for material of historical interest in the attic of the "geology laboratory" (now Old Chapel), where various items had earlier been found. He wrote,

> *We foolishly believed that we had pretty well exhausted the attic of all its treasure ... We began to fumble in the depths of the tray which contained [old diplomas], casting out several dozen bricks and a thick mortar of dust by way of making a beginning. Under the bricks there appeared a large collection of classroom maps on wooden rolls ... After removing a strata of legal papers ... we came upon a battered portfolio, its green cover granulated with age. We knew that we had never seen it before, so we pulled it out of its hide-a-way and spread it open on an improvised desk of packing boxes under the skylight.*[2]

Hislop had discovered the long-forgotten drawings of Joseph Ramée, made in 1813, for the Union College campus. Ramée (1764-1842), a French architect and landscape planner, was by the twentieth century a nearly unknown figure in both Europe and America. (His life and career have only recently been reconstructed.[3]) He began his career in Paris but had to flee France during the French Revolution and spent most of the rest of his life moving from place to place, as a result of the wars and economic problems of this turbulent period in Europe. Having worked in Belgium, Denmark, and several cities and principalities in Germany, Ramée in 1812 came to the United States, where he spent four years, before returning to Germany and France. He produced important buildings and landscape designs in all the places where he lived, but because he never stayed anywhere very long, his work was often forgotten or attributed to other architects.

The campus plan for Union College was one of Ramée's most important works. Moreover, it was the most ambitious and innovative design for an American college or university campus up until that time. It was made possible by the grand plans of Eliphalet Nott, the dynamic young president of Union, who had decided to replace the existing college building, in the old part of Schenectady, with an expansive group of buildings on the large property he had acquired on a hill to the east of the town. In January of 1813, Nott met Ramée, who was traveling through New York State with David Parish, the man who had brought him to America, and Nott commissioned the French architect to plan his new college campus. Ramée worked on the design for at least the next year, mainly in Philadelphia, communicating with Nott by correspondence (usually through the multilingual David Parish), shipping drawings to Schenectady as he produced them, and returning to the college in May of 1813 and possibly again in 1814. The architect's commission totaled $1500, paid in three installments, from June 1813 to March 1815, which suggests that Ramée continued working on the project for about two years.

The portfolio discovered in 1932 constitutes the largest collection of Ramée's drawings anywhere, although it is only a portion of the drawings he must have produced for Union College.

Accompanying the portfolio was a five-page list (cat. 5), written in 1856 by Jonathan Pearson, a Union professor and at that time the college's treasurer.[4] Listed are about forty-five sheets of drawings, of which about ten were missing from the portfolio when it was found (the exact numbers are uncertain for a variety of reasons).[5] The surviving drawings are now preserved in the Special Collections, Schaffer Library, Union College.

The sheets range in size from approximately 9-by-11 inches to 23-by-34 inches. There are several types of paper, some bearing the watermarks of English and American papermakers. Many of the sheets have pinpricks in them, probably the result of measuring and subdividing distances with a compass. Some of the sheets have more than one drawing on them, and several have drawings on the reverse side as well. Altogether, there are about sixty-five individual drawings on the thirty-five surviving sheets. They include floor plans, elevations and section drawings of individual buildings, site plans showing groups of buildings, landscape designs, profiles of mouldings and other building parts, structural details, such as the wood-framing of roofs, and even full-scale drawings of odd-shaped bricks that were to be manufactured specially. They range from carefully finished drawings, drafted in ink, many with added watercolor, to rough freehand sketches in pencil, sometimes drawn in the margins next to more completed drawings.

Most of the sheets have identifying titles or other kinds of writing on them. Except for a few notations that may have been added by Jonathan Pearson in the 1850s, the writing is clearly original to the drawings. At least three styles of handwriting can be distinguished. One is recognizably the hand of Ramée, which we know from his surviving correspondence and other documents: a cursive, informal hand with distinctive forms of certain capital letters. In the Union drawings, this hand is seen in several marginal notations in pencil, mostly written in French, and in isolated identifying words, some in English, or in a hybrid French-English ("Chapell," "Galery"). In contrast, the main inscriptions, centered on the sheets and identifying the drawings ("Second Story of the President's House," etc.) are all in English and in more formal script, seemingly of two types. Although Ramée himself may have used different types of handwriting for different purposes, the multiple scripts suggest that he was aided by one or more persons in writing the titles after the drawings were completed.

Ramée no doubt executed most of the drawings in Philadelphia, where he was living during most of his time in America, and shipped them to President Nott. But Ramée would not have sent the rough sketches to Nott; he must have done these when he returned to Schenectady in May of 1813 and simply left them there. The result is that we have an unusually diverse documentation of an early American architectural design, in which we can see the full range of the design process, from initial conceptual sketches to final drawings.

The drawings that have survived, however, are only part of what Ramée must have produced and delivered to President Nott. In fact, some of the buildings the architect designed are not represented at all in the drawings that survive. The reason for this is suggested by the fact that of these surviving drawings, nearly all show buildings that were not constructed, while the buildings that were constructed—notably North and South Colleges—are not represented. This makes sense, because in the case of the built structures, the drawings would have been used in the construction process, by the contractor and others, and could easily have been damaged and lost. Drawings for the unbuilt structures were more likely to have been kept intact in a college office.

One of the missing drawings is especially intriguing. This is the first one on Pearson's list, described as "A large view (hanging in Treasurers Office) of all the buildings & foreground." The Treasurer's Office was Pearson's own office. This was almost certainly a watercolor perspective rendering of the final design. Ramée was perhaps the most skilled architectural renderer working in America at this time, as can be seen in his exquisite perspective drawing for the Baltimore Washington Monument competition, also of 1813 (*fig. 1*).[6]

We can get an idea of what Ramée's rendering of the Union design looked like from two images that were made soon afterwards: an engraving produced in Albany about 1818, called the Klein engraving (cat. 1); and a painting by a Schenectady resident named William Givens (cat. 2). Both images portray Ramée's design for the campus, and both show it in perspective, but the differences in their perspective angles reveal that neither one was copied from, or even based on, the other.[7] They must have been representations of two separate perspective drawings by Ramée. They also present slightly different versions of the campus plan—in particular showing different types of landscaping. The source of the Klein engraving was probably the drawing by Ramée that Pearson designated number one on his list.[8]

Both the Klein engraving and the Givens painting reveal the basic components of Ramée's final design for the Union campus. Buildings are arranged to form an immense courtyard, six hundred feet in width and open toward the west. Linking many of the buildings are arcaded structures, one of which forms a semicircle at the back of the court. In the center of the space is a domed rotunda, intended as the college chapel. Surrounding the buildings are extensive landscaped grounds, in various styles of garden design. The architecture of the buildings is in an extremely simplified form of neoclassicism, reminiscent of the radical designs of Claude-Nicolas Ledoux, who had influenced the young Ramée during his training in Paris. Even traditional classical columns are missing, except in the entrance portico of the rotunda. Otherwise, the buildings are composed of abstracted geometric forms—the only major feature that could be called decoration being the pattern of arches created by recessed panels in the wall surfaces that carry through the buildings and the connecting "colonnade" structures.

Some preliminary construction had been begun by President Nott before he hired Ramée. A stone retaining wall had been built (the Terrace Wall), to produce a level site on the hill, and foundations for two buildings had been constructed. Ramée was apparently told to incorporate

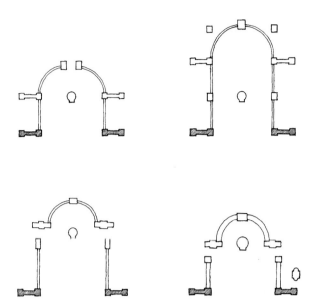

Fig. 2. Four of Ramée's site plans for Union College, redrawn to the same scale. The shaded buildings in each plan are North and South Colleges.
DRAWING BY AUTHOR

these foundations into his new plan, and these became North College and South College—the first buildings erected. As a result, in all of Ramée's preliminary site plans for the college, with their differing arrangements of buildings, North and South Colleges are the only buildings whose positions remain fixed (*fig. 2*).

Thirteen of Ramée's drawings form a puzzling group (cat. 6-18). Inscribed simply "Union College," they are floor plans, elevations, and section drawings of a large building that does not appear on any of Ramée's site plans of the entire campus. In fact, the building is incompatible with these plans, for its symmetrical and imposing form indicates that it was meant to be at the center of the campus, but there is no place for such a structure in the site plans. Moreover, the building was to contain nearly all the collegiate functions except the dormitories, which were always intended for North and South Colleges. In the central part of the building there is a library on the ground floor and a large chapel above; in one of the side wings are several classrooms, extra library space, and a "Society Room"; in the other wing is a private residence that was clearly to be the president's house.

These facts suggest that this large building was part of a plan for the campus that was very different from, and predated, the final design—a plan with only one main, central building and North and South Colleges. That it was earlier than the other plans is confirmed by the fact that the floor plans of the building are found, in fragmentary form, on the backs of two sheets of unrelated drawings (see cat. 17-18, 37-38); Ramée recycled these plans by cutting them to form sheets of different sizes to make new drawings. This large structure must be the building David

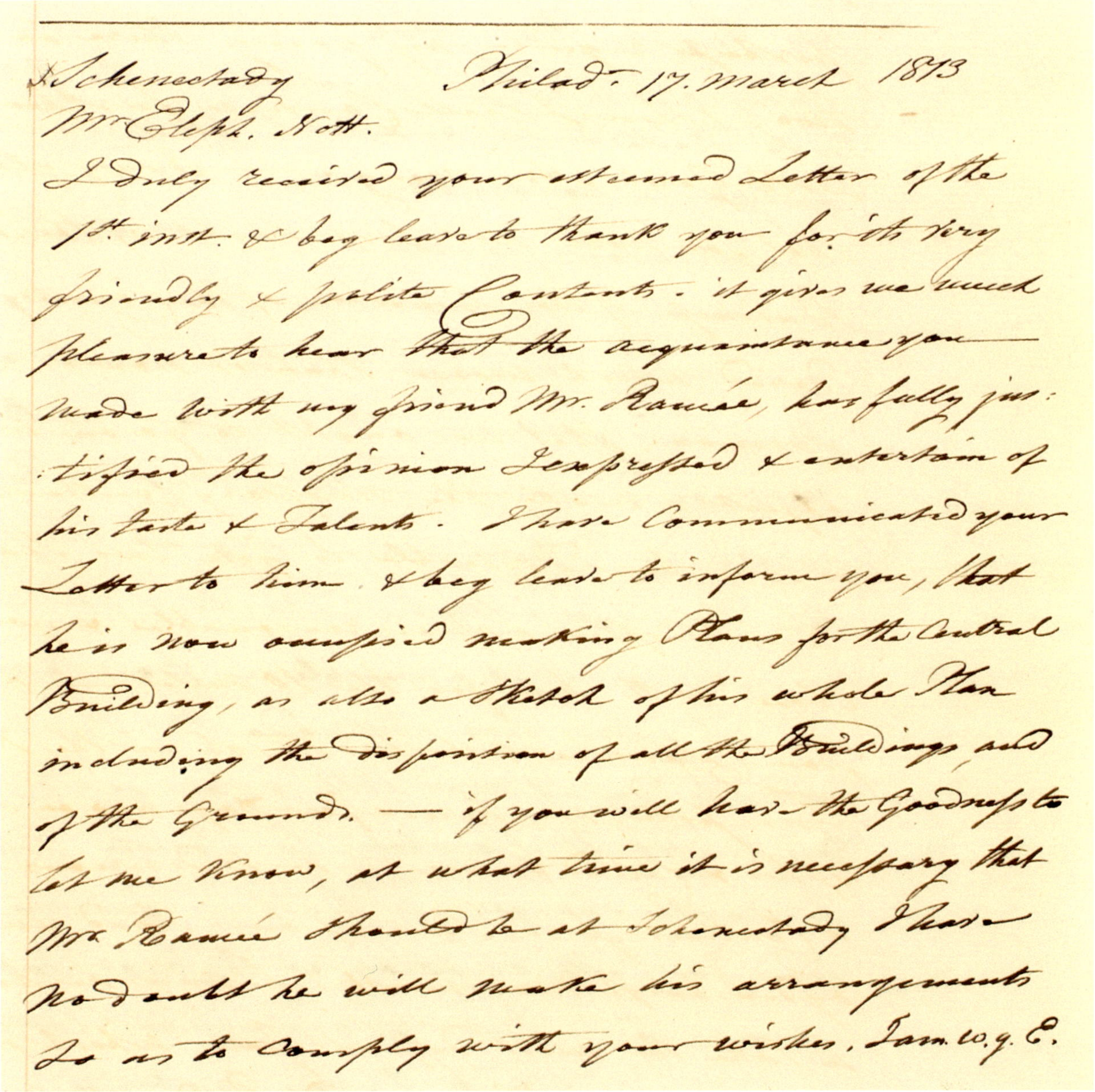

Fig. 3. Letter from David Parish to Eliphalet Nott, 17 March 1813. Copy in Parish's letter book.
COLLECTION OF THE NEW YORK HISTORICAL SOCIETY

Parish referred to in a letter of March 1813, when he reported to Nott from Philadelphia that Ramée was "making plans for the Central Building" (*fig. 3*).[9]

Ramée's first plan for the campus, therefore, consisted of this "Central Building" and the two dormitories, North and South Colleges. Ramée planned to connect the three structures by arcaded passageways, for the ends of two arcades can be seen at the edges of the elevation drawing of the Central Building (cat. 6). Was this building to be lined up with North and South Colleges, or set back? Positioned in a straight line, the buildings would have followed a pattern seen at other

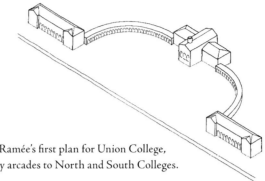

Fig. 4. Hypothetical reconstruction of Ramée's first plan for Union College, with the Central Building connected by arcades to North and South Colleges.
DRAWING BY AUTHOR

American colleges of the period (such as Yale), which was perhaps what Nott originally wanted. But Ramée would no doubt have preferred a more dynamic arrangement, with the Central Building set behind the line of the dormitories and the connecting arcades forming quarter-circles (*fig. 4*). In fact, this pattern is seen in one of Ramée's sketches (see cat. 19), as well as in parts of his final design for the college.

The drawings of this Central Building are detailed and carefully drafted, the type of "working drawings" used by builders for the construction of a building (comparable to blueprints in the modern period). Included are floor plans, front and rear elevation drawings, longitudinal and transverse section drawings, and plans showing the wood framing of the two floors. Ramée surely drafted similar drawings for North and South Colleges, but none of these survive.

When Ramée returned to Schenectady in May of 1813, he must have presented his plans for the Central Building to President Nott. Something at this time led to a rethinking of the entire design and a decision to make a more ambitious plan, unprecedented in American architecture. Perhaps Nott realized that one central building and two dormitories could not contain all the functions he envisioned for the college. This was the period of Nott's greatest optimism about the future of his institution. He was successfully lobbying the New York State Legislature for authority to raise large sums of money through public lotteries, he was planning additional purchases of land in order to enlarge the college site, and he thought he could plan on a grand scale, which ultimately proved to be unrealistic.

Ramée no doubt encouraged Nott's optimism. All architects naturally like ambitious plans, and in this case, increasing the number of buildings would allow Ramée greater potential for the creation of architectural and spatial effects. It presented, in fact, an opportunity Ramée had never before had, to explore arrangements of many buildings and spaces—the types of compositions favored by French architects of this period.

In his new plan for the college, Ramée in effect disassembled the previous Central Building, turning its component parts into separate buildings. The chapel became a rotunda and remained at the center of the campus. The classrooms, president's residence, and other functions became separate structures around the periphery of the central courtyard. And additional facilities were provided in the arcaded links between the buildings.

Four of the sheets of drawings found in 1932 show Ramée's exploration of various ways these new buildings could be related to one another (cat. 19-22). An additional site plan, too faintly drawn to be reproduced clearly, is found in sections on the backs of two sheets.[10] In all, there are nine identifiable site-plan variations shown on these sheets. The most complete of these, rendered in watercolor (cat. 22), corresponds quite closely, in its arrangement of the buildings, to the Klein engraving and Givens painting, so it probably represents the final design that Ramée presented to Nott. The other site plans fall into a sequence that leads logically to this final plan.[11] An additional drawing was discovered in Paris in 1890 (cat. 3), which Ramée had reproduced in his book *Parcs et jardins* in the 1830s (cat. 4).

All the plans show North and South Colleges in their fixed positions, and all have a circular building as the central focus of the composition. The plans that appear to be the earliest (such as cat. 21) are somewhat similar in pattern to the original Central Building plan, as if that original plan had been doubled to produce twice as many buildings. This then developed into an arrangement, represented by three or four of the drawings, having a large square courtyard with the rotunda at its center, and at its eastern end a large semicircle with a building at its center (for example, cat. 20). The next steps were to shift two of the large buildings toward the center of the plan, so they would not be hidden behind North and South Colleges and would play a more effective role in the composition, and to move the rotunda toward the back of the courtyard. These changes are found in the most detailed of these drawings (cat. 22), a site plan showing landscaping as well as buildings, carefully drawn in ink and watercolor—and with a last-minute revision on an overlay at the center of the plan.

One senses in Ramée's varied site plans—especially in the quickly sketched thumbnail plans drawn in the margins (such as those in cat. 19 and 20)—the architect's delight in exploring the possibilities of arranging many buildings and in working on a grand scale. This was the only commission Ramée received, as far as we know, that allowed him to conceive a large complex of buildings and to plan their overall layout as well as their individual forms. Indeed, it was perhaps the first group composition of this type in the United States.

Aside from the site plans, showing the arrangement of the buildings, most of the drawings are for individual buildings—floor plans, elevations, section drawings, and construction details. As noted earlier, the surviving drawings are mostly for buildings that were not constructed. These include the Central Building; the President's House (cat. 30-36); an unidentified building containing two lecture rooms (cat. 44); and the rotunda in the center of the campus. Some drawings do exist for the Colonnades (cat. 37-39), parts of which were built; and there are drawings for a "Steward's House" (cat. 41-43), which apparently were used in constructing

THE GRAND DESIGN 7

two dining halls, North Hall and South Hall, at opposite ends of the Terrace Wall—buildings which no longer exist.

The round chapel is a special case. The only drawings for it that survive are for miscellaneous details, such as door frames, mouldings, column capitals, and odd-shaped bricks (cat. 23-29), as well as a marginal sketch of the building and a faintly-drawn floor plan (cat. 19b, 20a). Several drawings for this structure, however, are included in Pearson's list but were missing when the drawings were found in 1932. They were described by Pearson as being floor plans, elevation drawings, and drawings of the entry doorway, the columns of the portico, and "dimensions of the timber for the cupola."[12]

On the back of the last page of Pearson's list is a penciled note: "16 drawings taken by Mr. Edward Potter to N.Y. June 3, to be returned." This was the architect Edward Tuckerman Potter, a grandson of President Nott, who was commissioned by Nott in the 1850s to construct the rotunda building. Potter is reported to have picked up Ramée's drawings for the building on June 3, 1858, and taken them to his New York office.[13] Using Ramée's concept of the rotunda simply as a starting point, Potter first produced a somewhat similar design, but it eventually developed into the up-to-date, High Victorian building that was constructed in the 1870s and later became known as the Nott Memorial. Potter apparently neglected to return some of the drawings to Pearson.

The distinctive characteristics of Ramée's simplified neoclassicism are seen especially in a watercolor elevation drawing of the President's House (cat. 30), which was intended to be at the mid-point of the curving arcade behind the rotunda. Traditional ornament has been almost completely eliminated, the design relying instead on the proportions of the parts and the play of geometric forms. The regular rhythm of arched recesses in the walls serves to unify the overall design, continuing from the façade of the house into the narrow arcaded structures connecting the buildings. (These structures are called "Colonnades" in Ramée's drawings, and this term has been perpetuated at Union.) The arcaded pattern is emphasized by the use of color, with the recessed sections of the walls given an earth-tone hue, contrasting with the creamy color of the surrounding walls. These color differences were to be achieved by adding pigments to the stucco or rough-cast that was applied to the brick walls of the structures.

These characteristics contribute to an impression of thin planes rather than massive forms—one of the most distinctive traits of Ramée's designs. Similar tendencies are seen in the work of other architects of this period, but Ramée took the trait to a remarkable degree, and the Union College buildings are among the best examples of it in American architecture of this time.

Another characteristic of Ramée's work seen in the Union College drawings is the importance given to landscape design. In Europe, Ramée had become known as a park and garden designer as well as an architect of buildings, and he had developed a conviction that a building should ideally be conceived as an integral part of its landscaped environment. He brought this notion to America, where it was largely unknown, and applied it to his work whenever possible. He included, for example, detailed designs for parks and gardens when he was commissioned to produce country houses, and incorporated trees into his design for the Washington Monument in Baltimore. (*fig. 1*) But the design of the Union College campus gave him the best opportunity to explore the concept and put it into effect. (See cat. 22, 36)

Ramée was skilled at producing various styles of landscape design, of both the geometric and irregular types, and his plans for the Union campus include examples of both. His personal preference, however, was for irregular, or "picturesque" landscapes, as seen in his most complete site plan of the campus (cat. 22), with winding roads, meandering streams, and informal groupings of trees around the central open spaces. When Ramée later included a plan of the Union design in his publication *Parcs et jardins*, he kept this general pattern for the main part of the campus, although he added more landscaped areas to the north (cat. 4).

One puzzling thing is that the Klein engraving and the Givens painting, both based on lost drawings by Ramée, show quite different types of landscaping. The painting has Ramée's preferred irregular landscape, while the engraving is predominantly formal, with regular rows of trees defining rectangular areas of ground. The most likely explanation for the discrepancy is that President Nott preferred formal landscaping (the informal type still being relatively unfamiliar in America at the beginning of the 19th century) and directed Ramée to include it in his final perspective rendering—on which the Klein engraving was based. If this rendering was also the drawing that hung in Jonathan Pearson's office, drawing number one on his list, it would explain an entry in his diary in which he described Ramée's landscaping as overly geometric and rigid (see cat. 1).[14]

Typical of Ramée's attention to the varied functions that landscape can have, he showed specific uses of it in his Union drawings. In his watercolor plan of the campus (cat. 22), several areas are shown as geometric patterns with linear rows, evidently vegetable gardens for the growing of produce. One of these, behind the President's House, was presumably to be used for President Nott's household. In the plan published in *Parcs et jardins* (cat. 4), at least one area seems to be intended for athletic exercise, and another for contemplation. But for Ramée, the main function of landscaping was to stimulate the appreciation and enjoyment of nature.

More than any other architect working in America at this time, Ramée incorporated sophisticated and diverse landscape planning into his architectural designs, and his campus plan for Union is the best example of this. The large informal park on the northern side of the campus, now known as Jackson's Garden, was begun shortly after Ramée produced his plans; although none of the architect's drawings shows it as it actually developed, it clearly was an outgrowth of this aspect of Ramée's design for the College. It is one of the finest and best preserved early picturesque parks in the United States.

Fig. 5. Drawing by Benjamin Henry Latrobe in a letter to Thomas Jefferson, 24 July 1817.
LIBRARY OF CONGRESS

If Ramée's Union College drawings had not survived, there would be no evidence of the importance of landscape in his conception of the campus. There would also be no evidence of the buildings that were not constructed, nor of how Ramée intended to use color in their surfaces. And there would be no way of knowing how the design of the campus evolved, from the relatively simple arrangement of three buildings along the Terrace Wall, to the complex final design, with many buildings connected by arcaded "colonnades"—creating dynamic spaces, in the center of which is the domed rotunda.

Without Ramée's drawings, we also would not be fully aware of the influence of the Union College design on later American architecture. In particular, Ramée's notion of a domed rotunda, as the centerpiece of a college campus, was unprecedented in America, and it appears to have contributed to Thomas Jefferson's planning of the University of Virginia. The influence came by way of the architect Benjamin Latrobe, who knew of the Union College design and in a letter of 1817 (*fig.* 5) gave Jefferson the idea of adding to his campus plan a large rotunda, which was to become the University of Virginia's most distinctive feature.[15]

The Union College drawings discovered in 1932 are invaluable historic documents, revealing one of the most significant architectural creations of early America. Many of them are also splendid examples of architectural drawing, ranging from freehand sketches to carefully drafted working drawings and watercolor renderings. Together they constitute a unique treasure in American architectural history.

1 View of Union College in the City of Schenectady/ After the Original Plan (the Klein engraving)

Also inscribed: "J. Klein, del't [i.e. delineator]... Wm Phelps, Printer... V. Balch, Sculpt [i.e., engraver], Alb'y."

22" x 32"

circa 1818

SPECIAL COLLECTIONS, SCHAFFER LIBRARY, UNION COLLEGE

This large engraving, which was produced about 1818 (judging from when the engraver and printer were in business in Albany) was probably commissioned by President Nott to publicize Ramée's design and promote its execution. The phrase "After the Original Plan," in the engraving's title, indicates that it was based on a drawing by Ramée.

The engraving can be compared with the painting by William C. Givens (cat. 2), which no doubt was based on a different drawing by Ramée, since the perspectives are structured differently in the two images. Another difference is in the landscaping, the engraving showing a predominantly formal landscape, while the painting has irregular or picturesque plantings—Ramée's preferred style of landscape. The most likely explanation for the discrepancy is that Nott preferred the more traditional, formal type of landscape and asked Ramée to use it in his principal perspective rendering, which Nott then had engraved.

The source of this engraving was probably the drawing that Jonathan Pearson designated number one on his list of the Ramée drawings (one of the items that was missing when the portfolio was found in 1932). Pearson described it as "A large view (hanging in Treasurers Office) of all the buildings & foreground." Since Pearson was the college's treasurer, this drawing would have provided his principal knowledge of Ramée's design of the campus. If it had the formal landscape shown in the Klein engraving, this would explain a curious criticism of Ramée's landscaping that Pearson wrote in his diary in 1855: "Remay ... laid out the grounds in true French style with broad straight avenues [of trees] ... No child could have conceived a worse and more inharmonious plan." Pearson, being more than a generation younger than Nott, would have preferred informal landscape, which by the mid-nineteenth century was the prevailing mode. And Pearson apparently did not realize that Ramée also had preferred the informal style.

The buildings in the engraving that are closest to the observer are North and South Colleges, the first structures to be built (in 1813-14), each having professors' houses in the pavilions at the ends and students' rooms in the middle. Extending east from North and South Colleges are the "colonnades" (constructed 1815), terminating in small structures (constructed in the 1850s), used for classrooms and other functions. Beyond them are structures similar to North and South Colleges and no doubt intended for additional student and faculty residences, which were never built. In the center of the campus is a Pantheon-like rotunda, to be the chapel. This building was not executed according to Ramée's design, but was the prototype for the sixteen-sided High Victorian structure now known as the Nott Memorial, constructed later in the 19th century. Behind the rotunda is a semicircular arcaded structure, at the center of which was to be the President's House. At the far left and right edges of the engraving are North and South Halls, dining facilities for the students, which were constructed in 1814-15 but no longer survive.

NOTES

[1] Codman Hislop, "The Ramée Plans," *Union Alumni Monthly*, December 1932, pp 48-53. Hislop had graduated from Union in 1931.

[2] Ibid., p 48. The building in which the drawings were found, Geological Hall, had been completed in 1856 and originally included the Treasurer's Office. Jonathan Pearson, the College's treasurer at that time, wrote the list of the drawings that was found with them, and it was probably he who put the portfolio in the attic of this building. The space was used for storing many Union College records and historical items.

[3] Paul V. Turner, *Joseph Ramée, International Architect of the Revolutionary Era*, Cambridge University Press, 1996. This is the source of much of the information about Ramée in this essay. The principal source of information specifically about Union College is Wayne Somers, ed., *Encyclopedia of Union College History*, Union College Press, 2003.

[4] "List of Plans drawn by Mr. Remay for Union College Buildings & Grounds. Aug 8/56 J. Pearson" The mistaken "Remay" is crossed out and corrected as "Ramée" (probably by someone after the portfolio was discovered in 1932).

[5] There are 42 numbered sheets on Pearson's list, bearing the numbers 1 to 43 (one of the sheets has two numbers, 25-26). At the end of the list Pearson wrote, "Besides 3 or 4 small drawings undetermined." Below this, Hislop wrote, "2 undetermined small drawings, 11/3/32"; in his *Union Alumni Monthly* article of December, 1932, Hislop described one these "undetermined" drawings as being "a very elaborate stable for eight horses …," which does not sound like any of the existing Ramée drawings. Below Hislop's note at the end of Pearson's list is another note (apparently added later by Hislop or someone else), giving the number 44 to a drawing described as "small amphitheater or lecture hall …," a drawing which does still exist. Within Pearson's list, Hislop noted ten of the sheets that were missing when he discovered the portfolio; another, sheet no. 36, is currently missing and it is not known whether Hislop simply neglected to note its absence or if something happened to it after 1932. For all these reasons, it is unclear exactly how many drawings were placed in the portfolio by Pearson in 1856 and how many of these were missing when it was discovered in 1932.

[6] Turner, *Joseph Ramée*, pp 218-23 and color plate 18.

[7] The reasons why the engraving and the painting must have been based on two separate drawings by Ramée are explained in Turner, *Joseph Ramée*, pp 202-03.

[8] See the description of cat. 1 (the Klein engraving).

[9] Turner, *Joseph Ramée*, p 194 and note 23. Letter from Parish to Nott, 17 March 1813 (New York Historical Society, *David Parish Letter Books*, book 4, p 211).

[10] The two halves of this site plan are on the backs of Pearson sheets numbers 13 and 14 (cat. 32 and 34). The plan is similar to the site plan of cat. 20, except that the central courtyard is longer (i.e., extends farther east). The President's House is indicated as being at the midpoint of the North Colonnade, to the side of the rotunda, rather than behind the rotunda, as in the final site plans.

[11] My hypothetical reconstruction of the order of execution of the site plans is as follows: 1. (cat. 19), plan in center of sheet. 2. (cat. 21), 3. (cat. 19), plan at left. 4. (cat. 19), plan at right. 5. The faintly-drawn site plan (not reproduced here) described in the previous note. 6. (cat. 20), plan in center. 7. (cat. 20), tiny sketch in upper right corner. 8. (cat. 22), original plan (under the overlay). 9. (cat. 22), overlay plan.

[12] Pearson's descriptions of these missing chapel drawings: "End view of Chapel (unfinished)" (Pearson list no. 9); "Front Elevation of the (circular) Chapel" (no. 10); "Plan of the Gallery of the circular Chapel" (no. 16); "First Story of the circular Chapel on the ground floor" (no. 17); "Interior view of the Circular Chapel" (no. 18); "Second Story of the Chapel being the first from the ground" (no. 19); "Dimensions of the timber for the cupola of the (circular) Chapel" (no. 20); "Size of the bricks to be used in the columns" (nos. 21, 22); "Sections of the columns & capitals" (no. 23); "Dimensions and profile of the Chapel Door under the Peristal" (no. 24). Numbers 21-23 are not specifically identified as being for the chapel, but only the chapel had columns. When Pearson put a description in quotation marks, it meant that he was giving the title that was on the drawing.

[13] See Mendel Mesick Cohen Architects, *The Nott Memorial, A Historic Structure Report*, Albany, 1973, p 26; Wayne Somers, ed., *Encyclopedia of Union College History*, Schenectady, 2003, pp 518-22.

[14] Turner, *Joseph Ramée*, pp 210-11.

[15] Turner, *Joseph Ramée*, pp 214-16.

Joseph Ramée's Drawings

2 Union College, Schenectady, N. York

William C. Givens

Oil on canvas

23" x 72"

Signed lower right, "Wm. C. Givens"

SPECIAL COLLECTIONS, SCHAFFER LIBRARY, UNION COLLEGE

This painting, like the Klein engraving, must have been based on a separate lost drawing by Ramée since, for one thing, the perspective angles in the painting are different from those in the engraving. Here the campus is viewed from a lower vantage point, closer to the way one would have seen it when approaching from the town of Schenectady.

William C. Givens (1794-1887) was of a hotel-owning family in Schenectady, and was apparently an amateur artist (no other evidence of his artistic work has been found). As noted in the description of the Klein engraving, the landscaping shown in this painting is largely informal, in contrast to the geometric landscape predominant in the engraving. The ground in front of the buildings is open lawn or pasture, allowing an unimpeded view of the college from the town—and also providing a sweeping view from the college to the Mohawk River and hills to the west.

One striking feature found only in the painting is the semi-circular ring of slender trees framing the rotunda. This was not an invention by Givens, for such a circle of trees is indicated in some of Ramée's site plans for the college (for example, cat. 3 and 21), and it is found in other designs by Ramée, such as his Washington Monument design for Baltimore (*fig. 1*). The feature was apparently in the drawing by Ramée that served as the basis of the Givens painting, but not in the drawing that was the source of the Klein engraving.

THE GRAND DESIGN

3 Plan of Union College

Inscribed in handwriting (at top and bottom of sheet) "Collège de l'Union à Schenectady, Etat de New Yorck, 1813."

Ink and wash on cream wove paper

9" x 11 ½"

SPECIAL COLLECTIONS, SCHAFFER LIBRARY, UNION COLLEGE

This drawing, which was found in 1890 by a Union alumnus in a print shop in Paris, is the only known drawing by Ramée for Union College that was not in the portfolio discovered in 1932. It is clearly the source of the almost identical lithographic plan that the architect included in his publication *Parcs et jardins*, of about 1839 (cat. 4). The drawing was probably made when Ramée was preparing this publication and standardizing the drawing style of the plans in it.

The campus design shown in this drawing is different in some ways from the earlier site plans (such as cat. 22), especially in having more extensive landscaping, but also in slight differences in the buildings. This raises the question of whether Ramée made these changes in the 1830s, while producing *Parcs et jardins*, or if they represent plans he had made in 1813 or 1814 while still working for President Nott. The architect often revised his plans when preparing them for publication (in his later years he published three collections of his architectural and landscape designs), and it is likely he would have wanted to show more extensive landscaped grounds, in the Union College plan, for his publication on parks and gardens.

At least some of the unique features of this plan, however, probably date to the original design of the college. The colonnades that extend eastward from North and South Colleges are similar in length to those that were actually constructed, in contrast to the longer colonnades shown in the other site plans. And there is an elliptical building, behind South Colonnade, which does not appear in any of the other site plans, but which is evidently the lecture-hall building shown in one of the drawings found in 1932 (cat. 44).

Additional landscaped areas are seen especially to the north of the campus buildings (the left side of the plan), where Jackson's Garden developed in the 1830s. A large area with rectangular strips of land was perhaps intended for agricultural cultivation, if not floral plantings. Another open area is divided into quadrants by paths, at the intersection of which is a cross-shaped monument, suggesting that the space had a memorial or cemetery function. And a long, narrow open area at the top of the plan may represent a running track. Surrounding these spaces and the rest of the campus are the winding roads, streams, and diverse groupings of trees that are typical of Ramée's picturesque style of park design.

This drawing also provides a clue to one of the mysteries about Ramée's life and career—what happened to his personal papers and drawings, very few of which survive. On his death in 1842, Ramée's architectural effects were surely acquired by his son, Daniel, also an architect. Daniel, who was married but had no children, died in Paris in 1887. The fact that this Union College drawing was found in a Paris shop in 1890 suggests that Daniel's widow may have disposed of her father-in-law's papers after her husband's death. Only the Union drawing is known to have survived this disposition.

4 Plate 13 of Ramées *Parcs et jardins, composés et exécutés dans différentes contrées de l'Europe et des États unis d'Amérique*

Lithograph

Paris, circa 1839

Inscribed: "College de l'union à Schenectady, Etat de Neu-York. Ramée 1813."

10" x 14"

SPECIAL COLLECTIONS, SCHAFFER LIBRARY, UNION COLLEGE

The publication *Parcs et jardins* consists of nineteen lithographic plans of Ramée's designs for parks and landscaped estates, ranging over four decades of his career, in Germany, Denmark, the United States, Belgium, and France. All of the plans follow a consistent format and style of drawing, revealing that Ramée redrew the plans for these projects in preparing the publication. The drawing of the Union College design (cat. 3) is the only one of these preparatory drawings that survives.

Parcs et jardins, like Ramée's other two publications, is extremely rare. Only two copies of it are known, one of which was acquired by Union College in 1956.

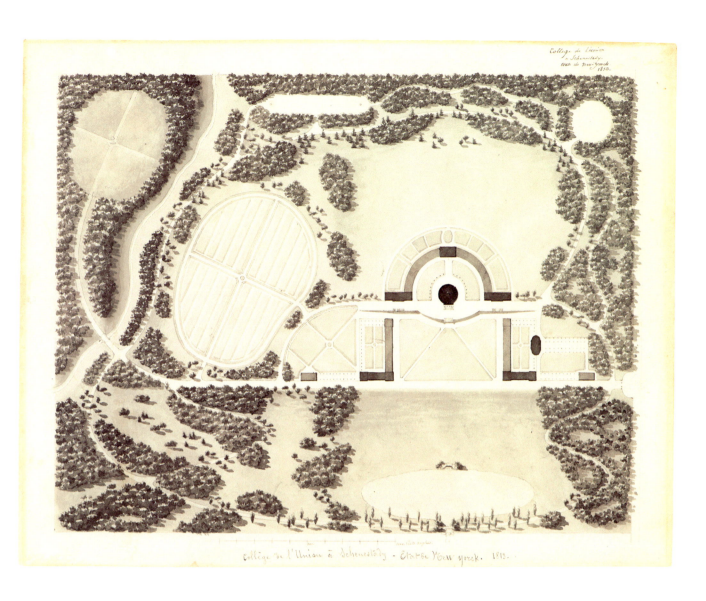

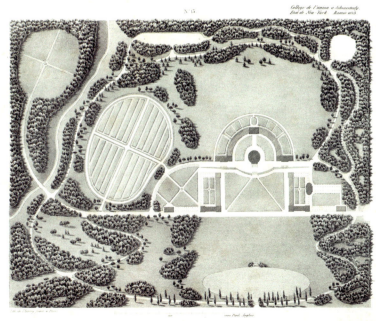

THE GRAND DESIGN 17

List of Plans drawn by
Mr. Remay [Ramée] for Union College
Buildings & Grounds.   Aug 8/56
                        J. Pearson

1. A Large view (hanging in Treasurers Office) of all the buildings & foreground.
   (missing 1/3/32 - C.H.)

2. A plan of the Grounds immediately surrounding the Buildings in which Phil. Hall & Geol. Hall are called "Small Colleges." (missing 1/3/32 - C.H.)

3. A Section of the Chapel showing timber Roof &c

4. A Side Elevation and Section of the Chapel &c.

5. A Back Elevation of the Chapel.

6. Front Elevation of Chapel
   Note. 3. 4. 5 & 6. are drawing of a <u>rectangular</u> Building with wings.

7. Detached plan of a garden (back of Presidents house?)

5 Jonathan Pearson's List, dated 8 August 1856

Pen and brown ink on cream laid paper, blind stamped upper left. (Garcon's Congress)

12 ¾" x 7 ¾" (5 pages)

SPECIAL COLLECTIONS, SCHAFFER LIBRARY, UNION COLLEGE

This list was included with the drawings that were discovered in 1932 in a portfolio in the attic of Old Chapel at the College. The first page is headed "List of Plans drawn by Mr. Remay for Union College Buildings & Grounds. Aug 8/56 J. Pearson." The name "Remay" is crossed out and corrected as "Ramée," probably by someone after the portfolio was found in 1932. The fact that Pearson did not know how the architect's name was spelled suggests that he knew about Ramée only from conversation with President Nott. None of the Union College drawings that were available to Pearson bore the architect's name.

THE GRAND DESIGN 19

CENTRAL BUILDING DRAWINGS

6 Central Building
Front elevation

Pearson #6

Black ink and transparent watercolor over faint graphite and compass pinpricks, with brown ink inscription; red crayon pencil numbering on cream wove paper with "J. WATMAN 1802."

21 ⅞" x 38"

SPECIAL COLLECTIONS, SCHAFFER LIBRARY, UNION COLLEGE

This is one of thirteen sheets that show a large building (about 200 feet wide, according to the scale), titled simply "Union College," which does not appear in any of Ramée's site plans. Various types of evidence reveal that the building was part of the architect's first plan for the college—the "Central Building" that Ramée was designing in March of 1813, according to a letter from David Parish to President Nott. This Central Building was to contain nearly all the college functions (including chapel, library, classrooms, and even the president's house), except for the students' rooms, and it was surely intended to be positioned between North and South Colleges.

This front elevation shows arches at the edges of the building, indicating that arcaded colonnades would connect the building to North and South Colleges. An arrangement of buildings in a straight line was found at other American colleges of this period, but Ramée would no doubt have preferred a more dynamic pattern, placing the Central Building behind and connecting it to North and South Colleges with semicircular arcades. (See *fig. 4*, page 6 of essay) This pattern is in fact shown in a rough sketch plan on Pearson sheet 22-verso (cat. 19), a sketch Ramée probably made when he was first considering a more ambitious design for the Union campus.

Jonathan Pearson, in his list of the drawings, identifies this Central Building with various names, including "Rectangular Chapel," to distinguish it from the "Circular Chapel," the rotunda. Pearson was perhaps unaware that this "Rectangular Chapel" building was part of Ramée's first plan for the campus, which was superseded by the final plan, with its circular chapel.

The design of the building's façade is somewhat puzzling, as it is not typical of Ramée's radically simplified neoclassicism. More conservative or traditional features include the rusticated lower story and the Ionic pilasters on the projecting central section, framing Palladian windows. One might suspect that the design was the work of a different architect; but Ramée's distinctive handwriting appears on some of the drawings for the building, and some of its other features are fully typical of his work. Perhaps Ramée was initially constrained by certain requirements made by President Nott, before the architect convinced him to move in more innovative directions.

7 Central Building
Rear elevation

Pearson #5

Black ink over faint graphite and compass pinpricks with brown ink inscription on cream wove paper.

22 ¼" x 34"

SPECIAL COLLECTIONS, SCHAFFER LIBRARY, UNION COLLEGE

The design of the rear elevation is simpler than that of the main façade, having no classical columns or pilasters with capitals. The second story of the central section of the building simply has arched recesses in the wall—similar to the pattern the architect later used for the Union College buildings, such as North and South Colleges. There are no windows in these recesses, for the chapel, which is directly behind this wall on the second story, is lit only from above.

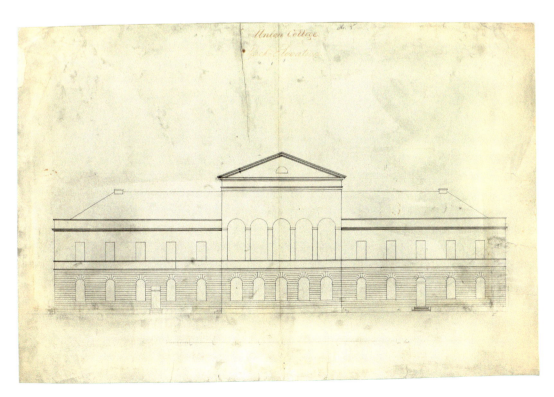

THE GRAND DESIGN 21

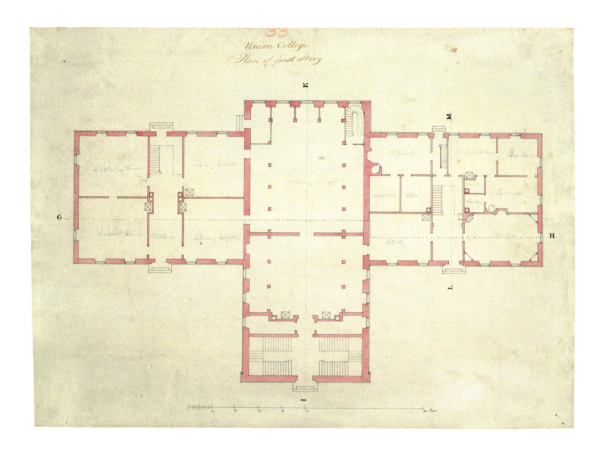

8 Central Building
First story plan

Pearson #33

Black ink and transparent watercolor over faint graphite and compass pinpricks with brown ink inscription; red crayon pencil numbering on cream wove paper.

16 ⅜" x 22 ⅝"

SPECIAL COLLECTIONS, SCHAFFER LIBRARY, UNION COLLEGE

In this floor plan, as well as the plan of the second floor, the functions of the rooms are written in pencil in a hand that does not appear to be Ramée's, but the designations were apparently made at the time the design was made. The three sections of the building have distinct functions and separate entrances. In the central section, the entrance is into a stair hall that leads up to the chapel, the principal space in the building; beyond the stairs, on the ground floor, is a large lobby or reception hall; beyond this is the main library space, designated "Library Large."

The wing on the left (north) side of the building is devoted to various academic uses. Two rooms, designated "Library Small," have access to the main library space; on the other side of a hallway are a "Recitation Room" and "Society Room." On the second floor in this wing, one room is labeled "Lecture," another "Apparatus" (evidently for science instruction), and two are left unidentified.

The wing on the right (south) side of the building is a private residence, surely for the college president. The rooms at the front are a "Parlour" and a "Study" (with a door giving access to the central section of the building and the college library). The central hallway leads, on the left side of the house, to a "Kitchen," "Cookroom," and "Store." On the right side, the hallway gives access to a room designated "Breakfast Room," which in turn leads to two rooms labeled "Bed Room" and two small "Pantry" spaces. It is odd that there is no room called a dining room. The two bedrooms accessible only through the "Breakfast Room" were perhaps meant to be for servants.

An unusual fact about the floor plans of this building is that only two of rooms are shown with fireplaces (the parlor and kitchen in the president's house), while most of the rooms have rectangular objects that are apparently space-heating stoves. Eliphalet Nott was very interested in the technology of heating with stoves and had invented several types of them. By coincidence, Ramée also was interested in room-heating stoves and had designed several for houses in both Europe and the United States. The college president and the architect no doubt conferred about their mutual interest in heating and decided to depend largely on heating the Union College buildings with stoves rather than fireplaces. Some of Ramée's later plans for the college, however, have a more equal use of fireplaces and room-heating stoves.

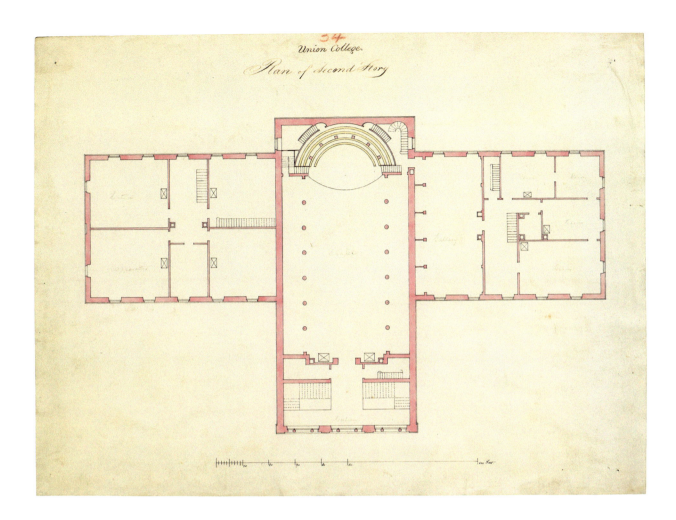

9 Central Building
Second story plan

Pearson #34

Black ink and transparent watercolor over faint graphite and compass pinpricks with brown ink inscription; red crayon pencil numbering on cream wove paper.

16 ¾" x 22 ⅞"

SPECIAL COLLECTIONS, SCHAFFER LIBRARY, UNION COLLEGE

On the second floor, the central section of the building is devoted completely to the college chapel (along with the stairway leading up it from the building's entrance). A row of six columns is on each side of the chapel, supporting a balcony or gallery above. At the east end of the space is a raised area, presumably for an altar, containing a semicircular row of piers which support arches, and above them a half-dome, creating an apsidal space. (Understanding these forms requires examining the section drawings of the building as well as the floor plans.) Narrow stairways around the perimeter of this apse space give access to the raised altar level and the balconies above; one stair, in the southeast corner, leads down to the library on the first floor. The main space of the chapel has a vaulted ceiling, in the center of which is an open structure, or "lantern," which rises through the roof and is the only source of light for the chapel.

The wing on the northern side of the building has additional academic spaces on this second floor. On the southern side is the upper floor of the president's house, with four rooms simply labeled "Room"—no doubt bedrooms. However, a large area of this second floor of the president's house is devoted to a room of uncertain function: designated "Gallery," it has access both to the hallway in the president's house and to the apse area of the chapel. It is not a gallery in the sense of providing additional space for a congregation, for it is not open to the chapel. Perhaps it was intended as an exhibition gallery, or a lecture hall for the president's use.

Two tones of watercolor are used on this plan. As in the first-floor plan, red is used to show walls, piers, and columns. A light brown or yellow tone is used to show semicircular rows of benches in the apse area of the chapel.

THE GRAND DESIGN 23

10 Central Building
Longitudinal section

Pearson #3

Black ink and transparent watercolor over faint graphite and compass pinpricks with brown ink inscription; red crayon pencil numbering on cream wove paper.

23" x 33 ⅜"

SPECIAL COLLECTIONS, SCHAFFER LIBRARY, UNION COLLEGE

There are three section drawings of this building: this one, which is cut through the full length of the structure (a longitudinal section); one cut through the chapel lengthwise; and one cut through the narrow portion of the wing containing the president's house (a transverse section). The section illustrated here shows the form and spaces of the chapel, with its series of arches in the apse, its vaulted ceiling, and its open lantern at the top.

All three of the section drawings show structural components of the building in considerable detail, especially the timber framing of the floors, ceilings, and roofs. These were clearly "working drawings"—drawings to be used by the contractor in the process of constructing the building. If this Central Building had actually been executed, the drawings would probably not have survived. (Ramée must have made similar drawings for North and South Colleges.)

The reddish color is used for walls that are made of brick and are cut by the section. The light brown color indicates wooden structural members. Especially interesting is the way the vaulted ceiling of the chapel is shown, made up of short pieces of timber bolted together—a kind of prototype of laminated wood arches (see detail 10a). This is a structural system that was developed in France and Germany in the late 18th century (called the De l'Orme system in French, Bohlen-Dächer in German), which Ramée had used in several of his early buildings. The system was largely unknown in the United States (Jefferson had encountered it in Paris and later asked the architect Benjamin Latrobe to use it for parts of the U.S. Capitol Building); its presence in this section drawing for the Central Building at Union College is one bit of internal evidence that Ramée was indeed the architect of this design.

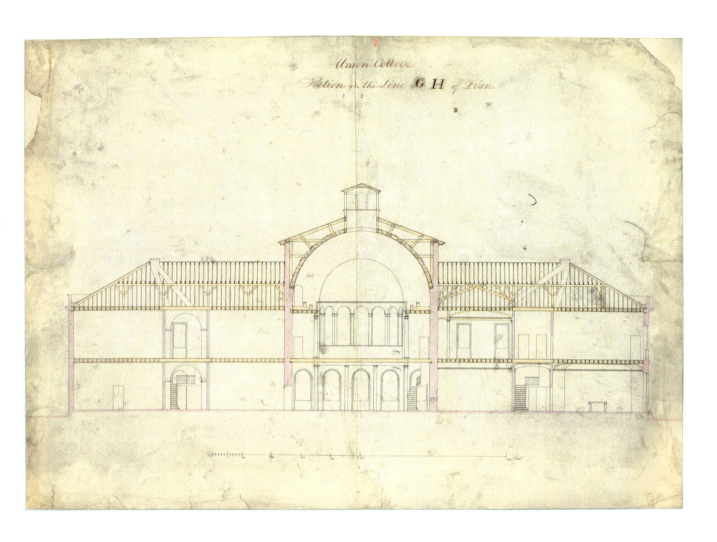

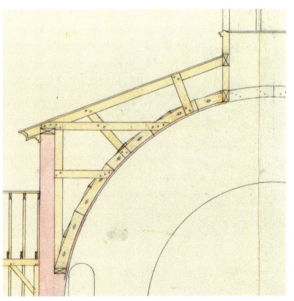

Detail 10a, showing wooden structure of vaulted ceiling in chapel.

THE GRAND DESIGN

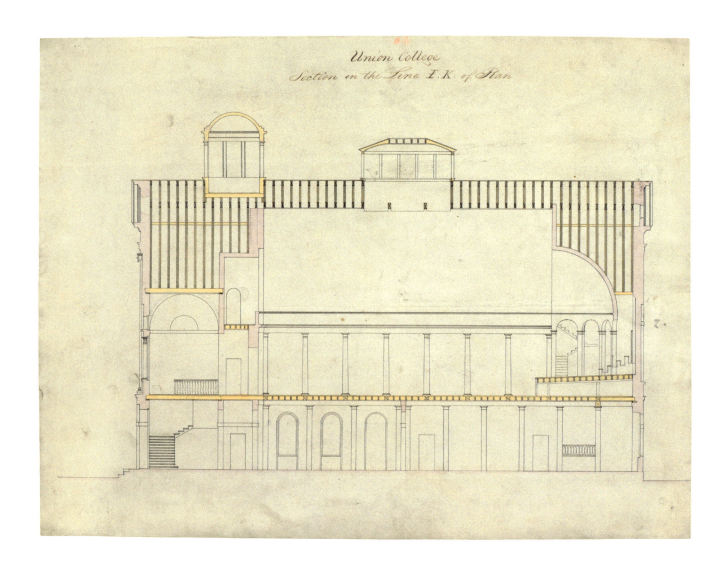

11 Central Building

Longitudinal section through chapel

Pearson #40

Black ink and transparent watercolor over faint graphite and compass pinpricks with brown ink inscription; red crayon pencil numbering on cream wove paper.

16 9/16" x 22 5/16"

SPECIAL COLLECTIONS, SCHAFFER LIBRARY, UNION COLLEGE

This section drawing, cut through the chapel lengthwise, shows several features not seen in the previous section. Among them are the semi-spherical vault at the east end of the chapel (to the right in this drawing), the spatial character of this apse area, the cupola on the roof at the western end of the building, and the configuration of spaces on the three floor levels beneath this cupola. We also see that the lantern atop the chapel is longer in the east-west direction than in the north-south direction (as seen in the previous section drawing).

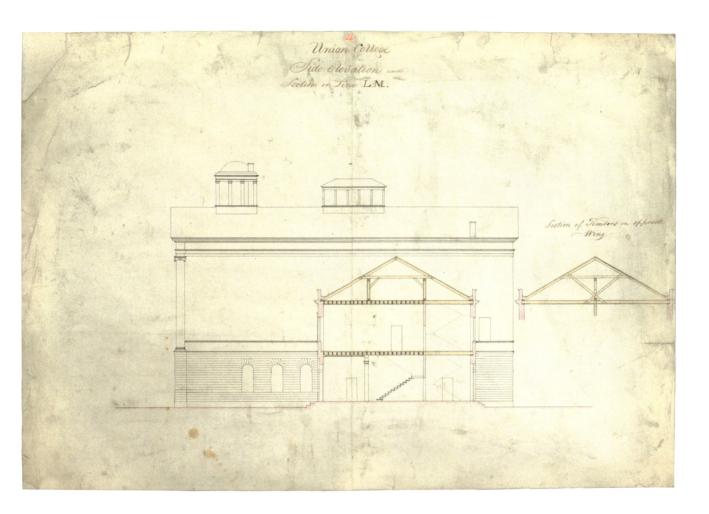

12 Central Building

Side elevation of chapel and transverse section through south wing of building

Pearson #4

Black ink and transparent watercolor over faint graphite and compass pinpricks with brown ink inscription and red crayon pencil numbering on cream wove paper.

22 ⅞" x 33 ¾"

SPECIAL COLLECTIONS, SCHAFFER LIBRARY, UNION COLLEGE

This drawing combines a section through the south wing of the building (the president's house) and an elevation drawing of the side of the chapel as seen behind the section. On the right side of the sheet is an additional drawing, titled "Section of Timbers on opposite Wing," showing the roof structure of the north wing of the building. Ramée used different configurations of timbers for the roof structures of the two wings, presumably because the bearing walls in the wings were in different locations.

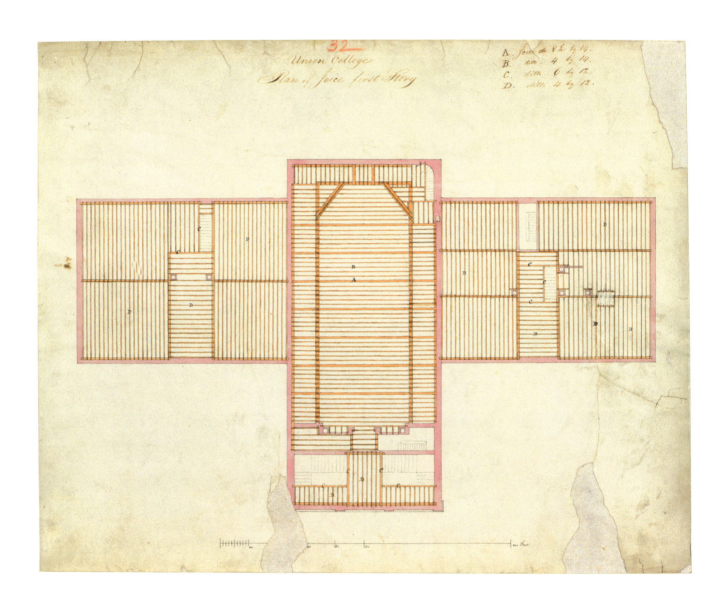

13 Central Building framing plan of First Story

Pearson #32

Black ink and transparent watercolor over faint graphite and compass pinpricks with brown ink inscription; red crayon pencil numbering on cream wove paper with "T G & CO" watermark.

17 ½" x 22 ¼"

SPECIAL COLLECTIONS, SCHAFFER LIBRARY, UNION COLLEGE

In these two plans, Ramée shows the configuration of the floor beams and joists in the building. The sheets are intended for the use of the contractor, in planning and executing the construction of the building. Even the dimension of each piece of timber is specified: letters in each part of the plan correspond to a list of dimensions on the upper right side of the sheet—for example, "C. Joice - 6 by 12 Inches." (The lumber sizes range from 4 by 8 to 8 by 14 inches.) This is the type of information provided by "specifications" in modern building practice.

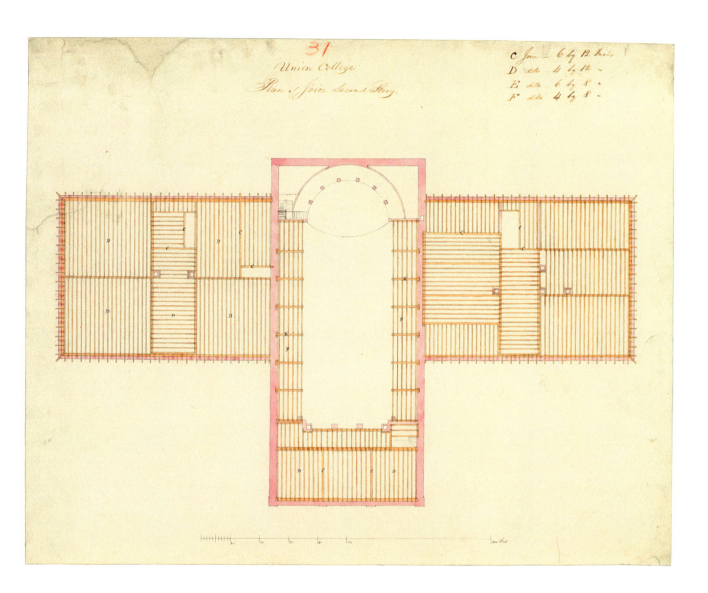

14 Central Building
framing plan of Second Story

Pearson #31

Black ink and transparent watercolor over faint graphite and compass pinpricks with brown ink inscription; red crayon pencil numbering on cream wove paper with "T G & CO" watermark.

17 ½" x 22 ½"

SPECIAL COLLECTIONS, SCHAFFER LIBRARY, UNION COLLEGE

15 Central Building extra first story plan

Pearson #38

Black ink and transparent watercolor over faint graphite and compass pinpricks with brown ink inscription; red crayon pencil numbering on cream wove paper with "T GILPIN &" watermark.

14 3/16" x 18 ¾"

SPECIAL COLLECTIONS, SCHAFFER LIBRARY, UNION COLLEGE

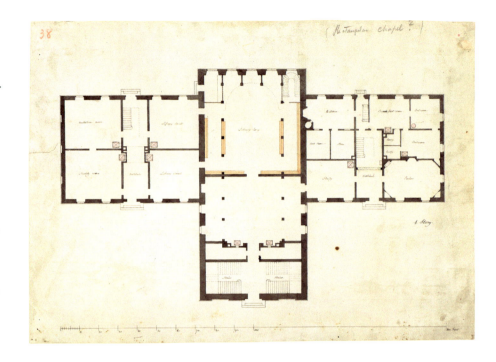

16 Central Building extra second story plan

Pearson #39

Black ink and transparent watercolor over faint graphite and compass pinpricks with brown ink inscription; red crayon pencil numbering on cream wove paper with "BRANDYWINE" watermark.

13 7/16" x 19"

SPECIAL COLLECTIONS, SCHAFFER LIBRARY, UNION COLLEGE

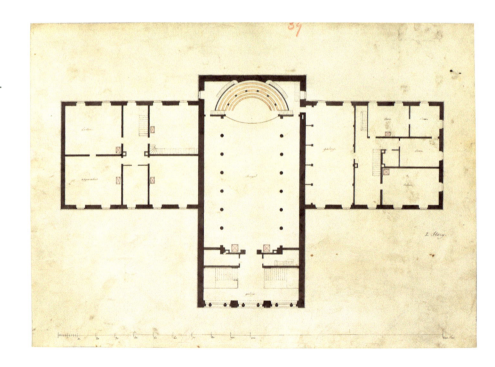

These floor plans are almost exactly the same as those seen in cat. 8 and 9 and are apparently preliminary versions of those plans. The lack of principal titles on the sheets indicates that Ramée did not consider the drawings finished. The only significant difference between them and the finished plans is that the preliminary plan for the first floor shows wall-like structures (colored light brown) in the library room, probably bookcases, which are not indicated in the corresponding finished plan.

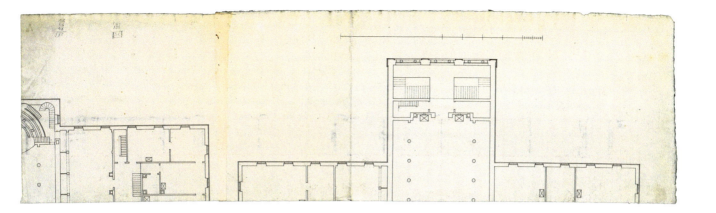

17 Central Building
fragments of floor plans

Pearson #8v (verso of cat. 37)

Black ink over faint graphite on cream wove paper with "T G & CO" watermark.

8 ⅞" x 31 ⅞"

SPECIAL COLLECTIONS, SCHAFFER LIBRARY,
UNION COLLEGE

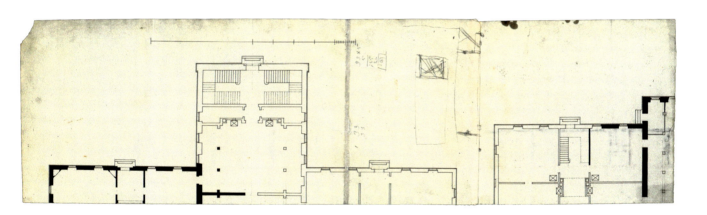

18 Central Building
fragments of floor plans

Pearson #12v (verso of cat. 38)

Black ink and transparent watercolor with faint graphite on cream wove paper with "T G & CO" watermark.

8 ½" x 31 ¼"

SPECIAL COLLECTIONS, SCHAFFER LIBRARY,
UNION COLLEGE

Each of these sheets consists of two pieces of paper, glued together, which had been cut from an unfinished floor plan of the Central Building. This was done to create long, narrow sheets which, when turned over, could be used for drawing plans of the colonnades—the long structures that extend eastward from North and South Colleges, in Ramée's new plan for the Union campus. (See cat. 37 and 38.) This recycling of paper by the architect is one of the pieces of evidence that the Central Building was part of his first plan for the campus.

THE GRAND DESIGN 31

SITE PLANS

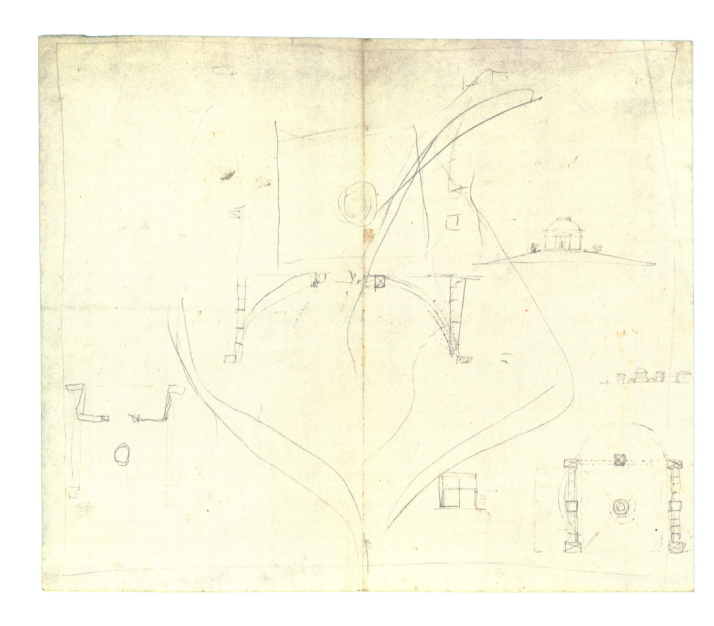

19 Sketches of site plans and rotunda

Pearson #22v (verso of cat. 27)

Graphite on cream wove paper.

13" x 15 ⅞"

SPECIAL COLLECTIONS, SCHAFFER LIBRARY, UNION COLLEGE

In the center of this sheet we see Ramée sketching a site plan in large, bold strokes. It is probably the earliest of the surviving site plans, done when the architect was in Schenectady in March, 1813, to present his plan for the Central Building to President Nott, but then proposed a greatly expanded version of the campus design. In the very center of the sheet Ramée drew the curving arcades that in the first plan connected the Central Building to North and South Colleges (see *fig. 4*), but the central space is now left open, giving access to a large courtyard beyond, dominated by a round building—the rotunda chapel that was to become the central feature of the campus. Ramée also indicated additional structures to the sides, the precursors of the colonnades and other buildings of the final design. We can imagine that Ramée may actually have sketched this plan as he met with Nott and described to him his new idea for the Union campus.

The significance of the large curving lines in the bottom half of the sheet is unclear. They might represent roads approaching the campus from the town of Schenectady to the west, but more likely they are unrelated to the site plan.

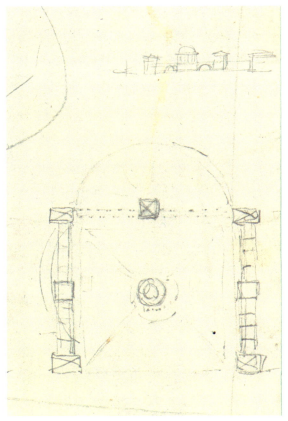

Detail 19a

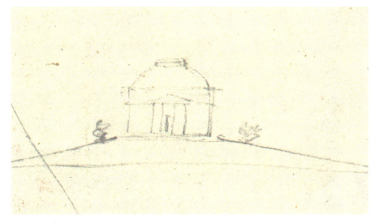

Detail 19b

We see Ramée developing his new concept of the site plan in two sketches in the lower left and right corners of the sheet. Especially significant is the drawing at the right (detail 19a), where attention is focused on the rectangular courtyard space with the rotunda at its center. The curving arms that originally connected North and South Colleges to the Central Building have now been moved to the rear of the complex—where they were to remain throughout the evolution of the design. Directly behind the rotunda is a square building connected to the sides of the courtyard by dotted lines, which probably represent an open arcade or colonnade, through which one could see the semicircular structures beyond. Ramée later revised this, moving the square building (the President's House) back to the mid-point of the semicircular colonnade. This small sketch plan can thus be seen as a pivotal stage in the development of Ramée's design for the campus.

Just above this site plan is a tiny elevation drawing (also seen in detail 19a), in which Ramée appears to be thinking of how this arrangement would appear to a viewer from the west—with the rotunda chapel now dominating the composition. This is apparently the architect's first drawing that shows how the rotunda would appear. Rather than having a pedimented portico, as did the later versions of the chapel, it shows a continuous series of columns around the periphery of the building.

Farther up, in the right margin of this sheet, Ramée sketched his revised version of the rotunda-chapel (detail 19b), now with columns only in a pedimented portico that serves as the entrance to the building. The structure is now raised on a mound of land, and trees are shown to the side, suggesting the semicircular ring of trees around the back of the rotunda that is indicated in some of the architect's later site plans and in the Givens painting.

THE GRAND DESIGN 33

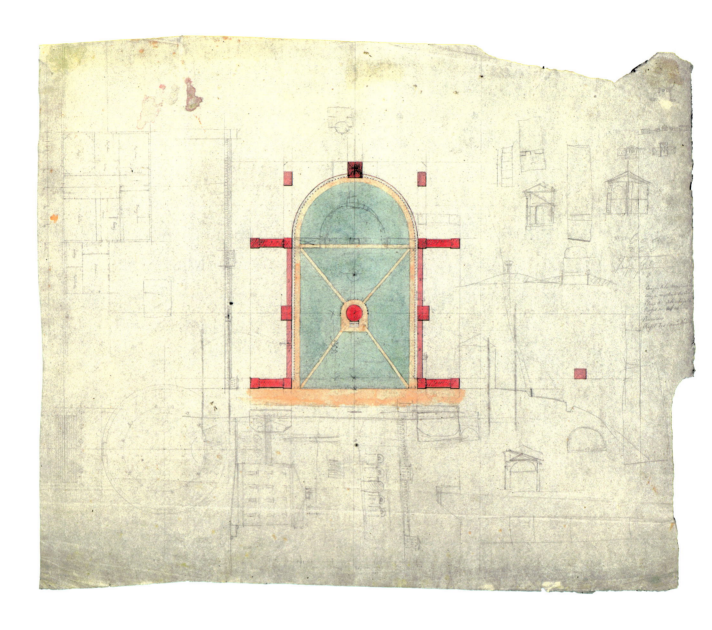

20 Site plan with marginal drawings

Pearson #25/26v
(verso of Catalogue number 40)

Graphite and transparent watercolor over compass pinpricks on textured cream wove handmade paper.

22 ¼" x 18"

SPECIAL COLLECTIONS, SCHAFFER LIBRARY, UNION COLLEGE

In the center of this sheet is a large site plan that probably represents the next step in the evolution of Ramée's campus design, following the site plans in catalogue numbers 19 and 20. North and South Colleges are still repeated, directly to the east (the upper part of the sheet), but pencil sketching, next to these buildings, shows Ramée revising the arrangement by shifting these additional colleges toward the center (so as not to hide them behind North and South Colleges) and reducing the size of the semicircular arcade connecting them to the square building at the eastern end of the composition (the president's house). Surrounding the back half of the rotunda is a series of dots, probably indicating trees, as shown in the Givens painting (cat. *2*).

The wide margins around this site plan are filled with numerous pencil drawings, no doubt made after Ramée decided the site plan was superseded and the sheet could be used for other purposes. These marginal drawings, some drafted and some sketched, show various aspects of Ramée's design, many of which are not found elsewhere in the surviving drawings. Four of the detailed areas are especially important; separate descriptions of them accompany their illustrations.

34   JOSEPH RAMÉE

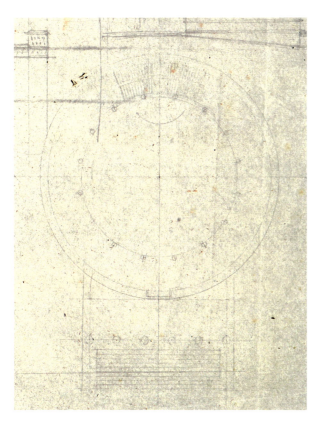
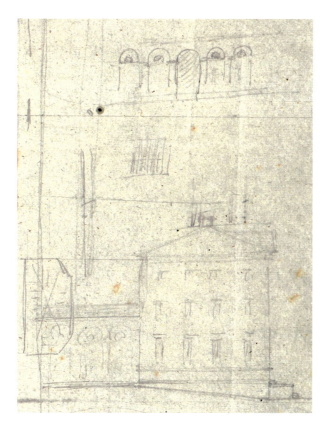

Detail 20a, lower left corner of the sheet.
Floor plan of the circular chapel. Drafted in pencil.

This faint drawing is the only floor plan of the rotunda that survives. It shows the chapel essentially as it appears in the Klein engraving and Givens painting, with a raised portico having six columns (hexastyle, in architectural terminology). Inside, the central space is ringed by sixteen columns, with a raised altar area opposite the entry. The circular space between the columns and the outer wall of the building is open to the central space, except for the part behind the altar, which is shown as stairways, apparently leading up to a balcony or gallery supported by the ring of columns. As in the Klein engraving, no windows are indicated in the wall of the building; the interior was to receive its only natural light from the oculus (with its surmounting lantern structure) at the top of the dome.

Detail 20b, lower left-central part of the sheet.
Side elevation of a three-story building, evidently South College, with part of the colonnade connected to it.

This largely freehand sketch is the only significant representation, in the surviving Ramée drawings, of North or South College. It shows the north side of the faculty residence at the north end of South College, with three bays of the arcaded Colonnade that extends east from it. The wall of the residence shows three floors, each with four windows, and the arched recesses in the Colonnade show semi-circular windows centered within the arches, just as these buildings were constructed. Above the drawing is another sketch of the Colonnade, in which one of the arched sections is drawn as if it was to be an open passageway into the courtyard behind South College.

Detail 20d, upper right corner of sheet.
Miscellaneous freehand sketches.

At the bottom of this detail is a rough sketch of the rotunda, showing it raised on an elevated mound. It is unclear whether the rounded mound drawn to the left represents a different way the land could be graded, or has some other significance.

Above are two section drawings that appear to show different versions of the colonnades. They can be compared with the section drawings in catalogue number 39.

In the uppermost area of the upper right corner of the sheet are several tiny thumbnail sketches of considerable interest. Two of them, an elevation drawing and a plan, show a large building that is different from any of the structures in Ramée's site plans (although it is somewhat reminiscent of the Central Building of the first scheme for the campus). Above this is a tiny perspective sketch showing North and South Colleges framing two curving structures that connect to buildings in the distance, with the rotunda in the center. Above this, in the damaged corner of the sheet, is a barely visible sketch showing a remarkable variation on this plan: the pattern of North and South Colleges, with the curving structures extending back toward the central rotunda, is mirrored on the far side of the rotunda, with additional curving structures. As with the immensely long colonnade on the other side of the sheet, one suspects that Ramée here was letting his fancy take flight and imagining grand possibilities.

Detail 20c, left margin of sheet, next to the central site plan. Elevation drawing of long colonnade.

In this sketch Ramée shows an amazingly extended version of the colonnades, consisting of over one hundred arched bays (in contrast to the twelve bays of the colonnade that was actually constructed), punctuated with a larger structure at the center of the range. The architect here is dreaming of a expansion of the project that must have exceeded the limits even of Eliphalet Nott's most ambitious plans for the college.

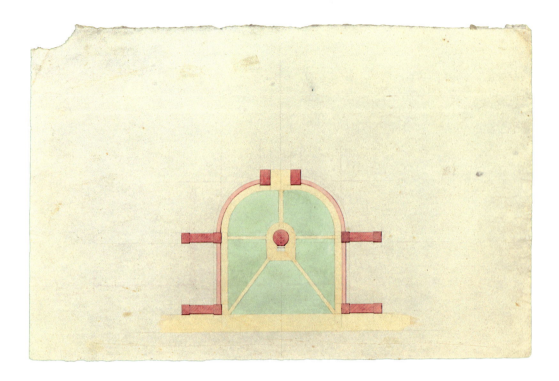

21 Site plan

Pearson #41v
(verso of cat. 39)

Transparent watercolor over faint graphite and compass pinpricks on cream wove paper.

11 ⅝" x 18"

SPECIAL COLLECTIONS, SCHAFFER LIBRARY, UNION COLLEGE

This drawing, with buildings shown in red, paths in yellow, and lawn in green, appears to be early in the evolution of the site plan for the campus. It may in fact be the first plan Ramée made, following the rough sketch (cat. 19) in which Ramée began moving away from the Central Building plan, toward a more dynamic design for the campus that involved complex spaces and many buildings. At the bottom of the drawing are North and South Colleges, but the Central Building, which stood between them in the first plan, has now been disassembled and its parts turned into separate structures. The chapel, the principal feature of the Central Building, has become a rotunda in the center of the campus; and the academic spaces and other functions in the Central Building have been placed in the colonnades and other structures around the periphery of the new courtyard. Ramée has also doubled, in a sense, the pattern of the Central Building plan: North and South Colleges are repeated to the east (in line with the rotunda), with the semicircular structures that connected them to the Central Building now leading to two rectangular structures. This was the beginning of a process of refinement that led to increasingly more integrated versions of the campus plan.

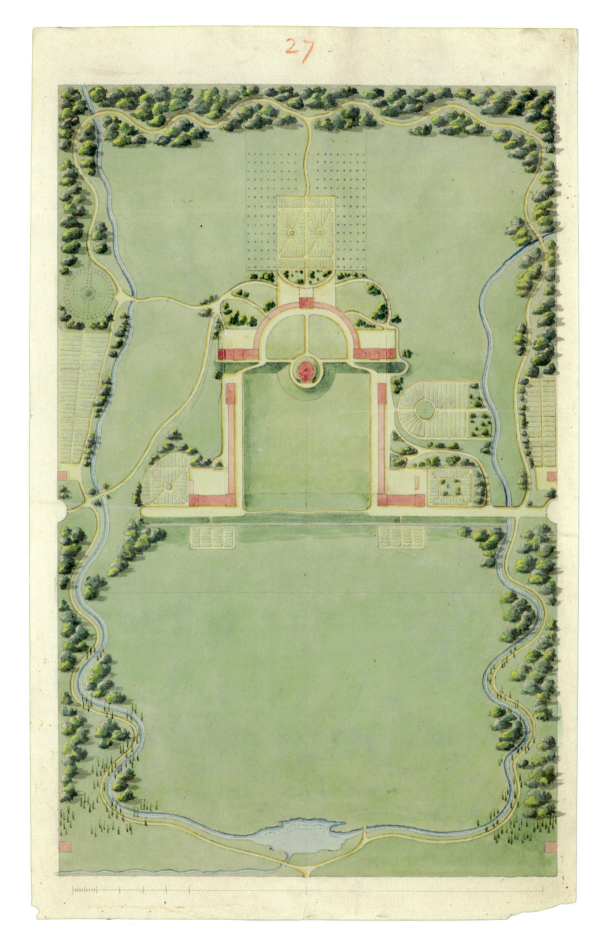

38 JOSEPH RAMÉE

22 Site plan of buildings and surrounding landscape

Pearson #27

Ink and watercolor; overlaid piece of paper glued onto center of sheet.

17 ½" x 11"

SPECIAL COLLECTIONS, SCHAFFER LIBRARY, UNION COLLEGE

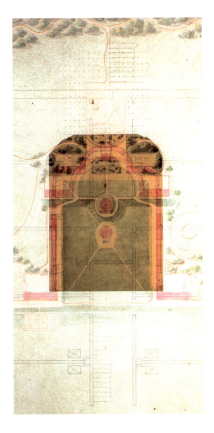

This colored site plan may be the most significant of Ramée's drawings for Union College. Besides its artistic appeal, it shows the architect's most complete design for the campus plan, and was no doubt made as a "presentation" drawing for the client, President Nott.

The positions of the buildings here are nearly the same as in the Klein engraving (cat. 1), which was based on a now-lost perspective rendering by Ramée; the arrangement of buildings represents the final stage in the evolution of the site plan. Remarkably, this watercolor drawing also reveals the last revision that was made in this evolution of the design. In the center of the sheet, the area around the rotunda was drawn on a piece of paper that was glued onto the sheet. By the use of a strong light it has been possible to discern the first design, under the overlay (see detail 22a). In this first plan, the central rectangular space is larger and the rotunda is in the center of it; in the final plan, on the overlay, the rotunda has been moved to the back of a slightly smaller rectangular space, and the semicircular arcade behind the rotunda has been enlarged and placed closer to the rotunda. In several respects this is a more integrated design, and Ramée apparently considered it his final plan for the campus.

Most significant about this drawing, however, is the attention it gives to landscape design. In Europe, Ramée had been successful as a designer of parks and gardens, as well as an architect of buildings, and he had developed distinctive views of landscape planning, which are evident in his design of the Union College campus. The landscaping here is largely in the informal, picturesque tradition, with irregular patterns of vegetation, but Ramée creates a great diversity of types of landscape within this general framework: broad open spaces at the center of the campus and toward the west (the bottom of the plan), allowing sweeping views both of the college and from it; winding pathways through groves of trees around the periphery; water features; geometric areas for agricultural cultivation, such as kitchen gardens behind the President's House (the eastern-most building in the plan) and near the two dining halls (set back from the northern and southern ends of the Terrace Wall); and more formal areas, such as the circular space on the upper left side of the plan—perhaps an area for contemplative meditation. For Ramée, landscaping ideally served many different functions, and the Union College design is one of the best examples of this in his work.

It was typical of Ramée, and of picturesque landscape planning in general, to include lakes and other water features whenever possible, in order to increase the diversity of natural phenomena. This often required changes in existing topographical conditions, and Ramée proposed this in the Union design, by diverting the courses of two streams, to the north and south of the central campus, so they would join and create a small lake directly to the west of the campus (the bottom of the plan). The stream to the north was Hans Groot's Kill, which still flows through this part of the campus—Jackson's Garden. The stream that Ramée shows to the south was apparently a diversion of Cow Horn Creek, which was in this part of Schenectady but no longer exists.

Ramée had developed in Europe a conviction that architecture was not complete until the landscaped environment around it had been created. He applied this principle to all his work in the United States (where the notion was nearly unknown at this time)—in private houses and estates, and well as public projects, such as his competition entry for the Washington Monument in Baltimore (*fig. 1*). The Union College design illustrates this principle best, and was perhaps the most advanced example of it in America at this time.

22a. Central portion of site plan, photographed to show both the plan on the overlay and the plan underneath it. The additional lines visible here are part of a floor plan that is on the back of the sheet (cat. 45).

THE GRAND DESIGN 39

ROTUNDA-CHAPEL

23 Detail of doorway, moldings, etc.

Pearson #24

Black ink over faint graphite; red crayon pencil numbering on cream wove paper.

19 ¾" x 17 11/16"

SPECIAL COLLECTIONS, SCHAFFER LIBRARY, UNION COLLEGE

On Jonathan Pearson's list of the Ramée drawings, about fourteen appear to be for the circular chapel, and about half of these were missing from the portfolio when it was discovered in 1932. In a couple of cases the identity of the building is unclear from Pearson's description, because he sometimes used the term "chapel" ambiguously, to refer either to the circular chapel or to the "rectangular chapel" in the Central Building. The missing drawings included floor plans, a front elevation, and a section drawing, and were probably among those borrowed by Edward T. Potter in 1858 for use in the design of the circular building that was eventually constructed, the Nott Memorial. The seven drawings that survive are for miscellaneous details of the chapel, intended as working drawings, to be used by the contractor if the building had been constructed following Ramée's plans.

In the title of this drawing, the words "Chapel door under the Peristal" must refer to the main entrance doorway of the building, behind the columns (peristyle) of the portico. The two doors and their framing are drawn in elevation, with profiles of the cornices shown to the right. The scale at the bottom indicates that the doorway was to be five feet in width.

In the right-hand margin is the word "chapell," in Ramée's handwriting. In contrast, the drawing's title may have been written by someone else.

40 JOSEPH RAMÉE

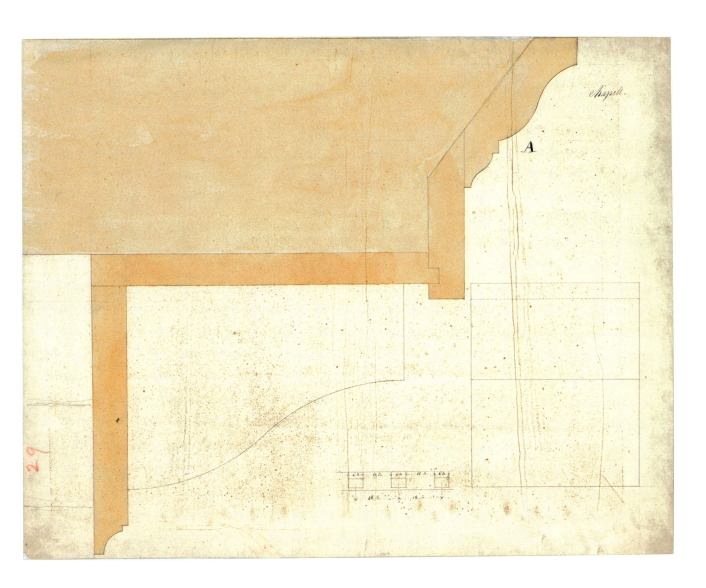

24 Detail of cornice

Pearson #29

Black ink and transparent watercolor over faint graphite; red crayon pencil numbering on cream textured wove paper.

18" x 23 ¼"

SPECIAL COLLECTIONS, SCHAFFER LIBRARY, UNION COLLEGE

This drawing shows the profile of a cornice or molding, but as the sheet bears no title, it is unclear what part of the building is represented. As in the previous drawing, the word "chapell" is written on the right side of the sheet, in Ramée's hand. The cornice is given a yellow-brown tone of watercolor—the color that Ramée normally used to represent wood.

25 Detail of pediment, and other forms

Pearson #28

Black ink and transparent watercolor over faint graphite on textured cream wove paper.

22 ⅝" x 17 ⅞"

SPECIAL COLLECTIONS, SCHAFFER LIBRARY, UNION COLLEGE

Here too, the sheet has no title but the word "chapell" is written in the margin. The drawing shows the corner of a pediment, presumably the pediment of the entrance portico. In the lower part of the sheet are profiles of two cornices, whose relationship to the pediment is unclear; these cornices are colored in a light reddish tone. As in most of these drawings of details, each item on the sheet is given a letter, which must have correlated to letters on the elevation and section drawings of the building, to show where each detail was located.

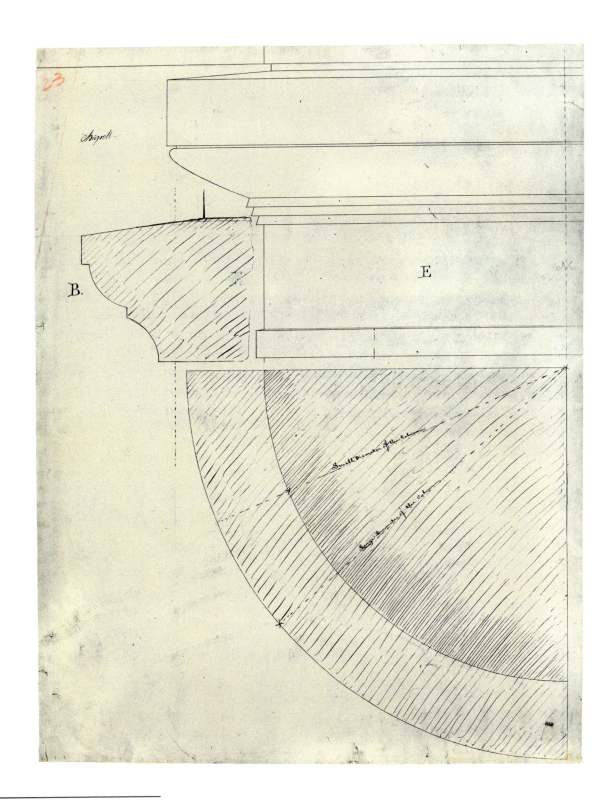

26 Detail of column and capital

Pearson #23

Black ink over faint graphite; red crayon pencil numbering on cream wove paper.

22 ¾" x 17 ⅞"

SPECIAL COLLECTIONS, SCHAFFER LIBRARY, UNION COLLEGE

Shown here are parts of one of the columns and its capital, in the entrance portico of the chapel. The sheet has no title, but again the word "chapell" appears in the margin. The column capital is in a variant of the Doric order, the simplest of the classical orders. Below the elevation drawing of the capital is the plan of the column shaft; since it was to be tapered, two dimensions for its diameter are given, labeled "Small Diameter of the Column" and "Large Diameter of the Column."

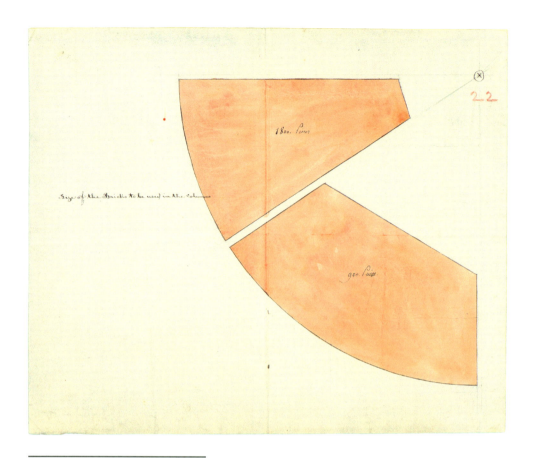

27 Detail of special-sized bricks

Pearson #22

Black ink and transparent watercolor over faint graphite and compass pinpricks with brown ink inscription; red crayon pencil numbering on antique laid paper.

13" x 15 ⅞"

SPECIAL COLLECTIONS, SCHAFFER LIBRARY, UNION COLLEGE

Each of these sheets shows two sizes of odd-shaped bricks that were to be manufactured specially for the construction of the columns of the chapel. (Like the rest of the brick surfaces in the Union College buildings, they would have been covered with a layer of rough-cast or stucco.) The bricks appear to be drawn full-scale, which would have been helpful to the contractor or brick manufacturer to whom the drawing would have been shown. The number of bricks required is also indicated: "900 Pieces" for one of the shapes, "1800 Pieces" for the other. The drawings on the two sheets appear at first to be identical, but in fact the bricks are slightly different in size and shape. Ramée apparently had to recalculate their dimensions and redraw them on a new sheet.

28 Detail of special-sized bricks

Pearson #21

Black ink and transparent watercolor over faint graphite and compass pinpricks with brown ink inscription; red crayon pencil numbering on antique laid paper.

12 ¾" x 5 9/16"

SPECIAL COLLECTIONS, SCHAFFER LIBRARY, UNION COLLEGE

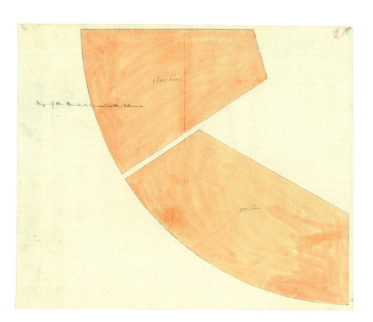

44 JOSEPH RAMÉE

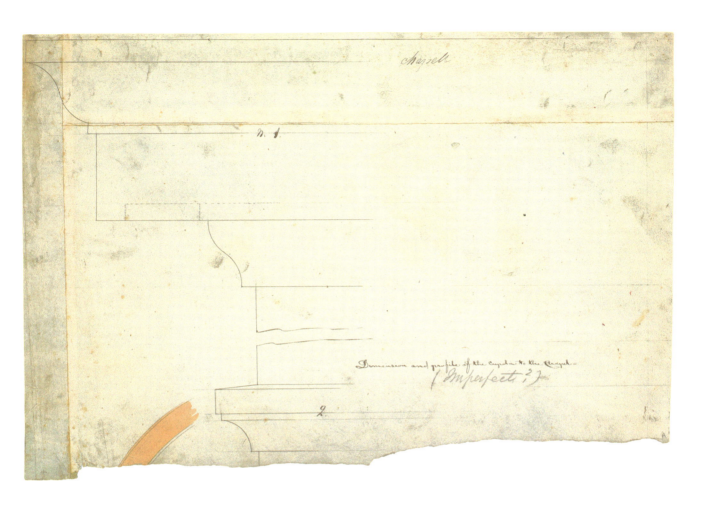

29 Detail of cornice

Not numbered by Pearson

Black ink and transparent watercolor over faint graphite on textured, cream wove paper. Paper extended top and left edge, bottom edge torn.

12 ⅜" x 18 ⅝"

SPECIAL COLLECTIONS, SCHAFFER LIBRARY, UNION COLLEGE

This drawing of a cornice or molding has the word "Chapell" written on it, in Ramée's hand, as do most of the other drawings of this building. Underneath the title, in pencil, is written "(Imperfect?)" in what looks like a later hand, perhaps Pearson's; its meaning is unclear. Also puzzling is a small drawing in the lower left corner of the sheet—a kind of arc, colored brown, which does not seem to be related to the main subject on the sheet.

THE GRAND DESIGN 45

PRESIDENT'S HOUSE

30 President's House
Elevation drawing of façade

Pearson #43

Black ink and transparent watercolor over faint graphite and compass pin-pricks with brown ink inscription; blue crayon pencil numbering on cream wove paper with "RUSE & TURNER 1807" watermark.

13 ¼" x 22 ⅜"

SPECIAL COLLECTIONS, SCHAFFER LIBRARY, UNION COLLEGE

The President's House was to be located directly behind the rotunda, connected to the rest of the campus buildings by a semicircular arcaded structure. This finely executed elevation drawing of the house shows portions of the connecting structure, with the arcaded pattern of recessed wall panels continuing through the lower part of the façade of the house.

The watercolor shows the hues Ramée intended for the walls of the Union College buildings: a light cream color for the main surfaces of the walls, and darker earth tones for the recessed portions that create the arcaded pattern. (The colors were apparently to be produced by pigments added to the rough-cast or stucco that was applied to the brick walls.) It is unclear whether the difference in color, in this drawing, between the recessed areas in the house and those in the connecting structures, was intended by Ramée to be executed, or simply shows him experimenting with different color possibilities. The blue-gray color applied to the roof presumably indicates slate.

The scale at the bottom of the drawing shows that the house was to be about 64 feet wide. Along with the watercolored site plan of the campus (cat. 22), this elevation drawing suggests Ramée's skill in architectural rendering.

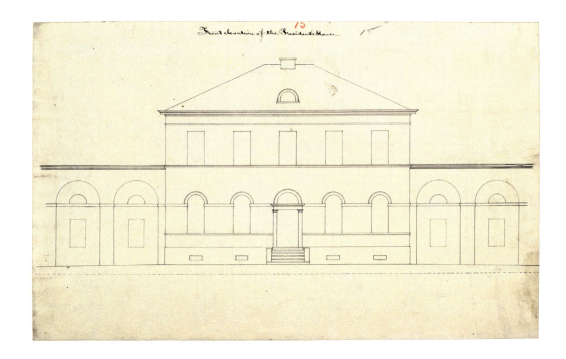

31 Presidents House
Additional elevation drawing

Pearson #15

Black ink over faint graphite and compass pinpricks; red crayon pencil numbering on cream wove paper.

10 ½" x 16 ¹⁵⁄₁₆"

SPECIAL COLLECTIONS, SCHAFFER LIBRARY,
UNION COLLEGE

This elevation must predate the preceding drawing, and not only because the preceding one is completed and thus presumably represents Ramée's final design for the house. More significant is the nature of the design itself. In this preliminary drawing, the lower part of the façade does not share the arcaded pattern of the colonnades on the sides, as it does in the completed drawing. In the process of planning the house, Ramée evidently came to realize that continuing this arcaded motif across the front of the house produced a more unified and integrated design.

THE GRAND DESIGN *47*

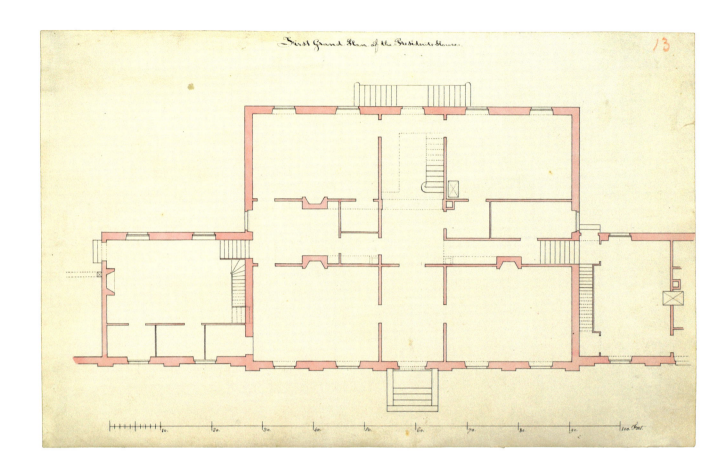

32 President's House
First story plan

Pearson #13

Black ink and transparent watercolor over faint graphite and compass pin-pricks with brown ink inscription; red crayon pencil numbering on cream wove paper with "RUSE & TURNER 1807" watermark.

11 11/16" x 18 7/8"

SPECIAL COLLECTIONS, SCHAFFER LIBRARY, UNION COLLEGE

The functions of the rooms are not indicated on the floor plans of this house, but it is likely that the two front rooms on the first floor were to be the parlor, on the right, and the study, on the left (following the pattern shown in the floor plans of the Central Building, where the president's residence was in one of the wings and the room functions were indicated). At the back of the house on this floor, a bedroom may have been on the right and the dining room on the left. If so, the room in the wing attached to the house on the left (part of the semicircular "colonnade") would have been the kitchen. The floor in this room is lower than in the main part of the house (the floors in the colonnades were close to the ground), allowing space for a low-ceilinged room on a second level above the kitchen, as shown on the second-floor plan. The corresponding rooms in the wing-colonnade on the right side of the house are of uncertain function. One difference between this president's house and the one that was in the Central Building is that most of the rooms here have fireplaces, with less use of room-heating stoves.

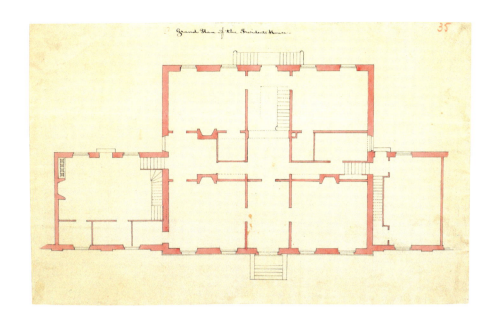

33 President's House
Additional first story plan

Pearson #35

Black ink and transparent watercolor over faint graphite and compass pinpricks with brown ink inscription; red crayon pencil numbering on cream wove paper.

10 ½" x 17"

SPECIAL COLLECTIONS, SCHAFFER LIBRARY, UNION COLLEGE

This floor plan and the preceding one are almost identical, so it is difficult to know which was earlier. However, several small clues suggest that this one was done first. In this plan, for example, a room-heating stove is very lightly sketched in pencil, in the room at the upper right corner of the house, while it is drafted fully in the other plan. Also noteworthy is the layout of the wing on the left side of the house. In this plan an object is shown, in the upper left corner of the wing, which seems to be a cooking stove—confirmation that this room was indeed the kitchen.

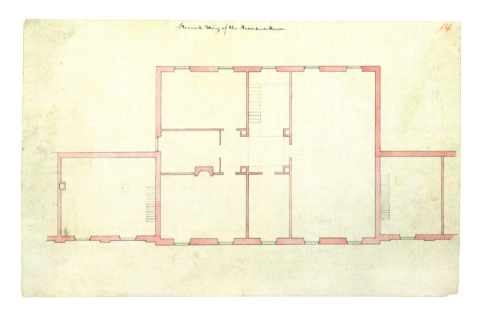

34 President's House
Second story plan

Pearson #14

Black ink and transparent watercolor over faint graphite and compass pinpricks with brown ink inscription; red crayon pencil numbering on cream wove paper.

11 ½" x 18 ¹³⁄₁₆"

SPECIAL COLLECTIONS, SCHAFFER LIBRARY, UNION COLLEGE

A puzzling feature of this floor plan is the large room on the right side of the house. One wonders if it might have been intended as a room in which President Nott could give lectures. A similar large room of uncertain function is on the second floor of the president's house in the Central Building (see cat. 9).

THE GRAND DESIGN

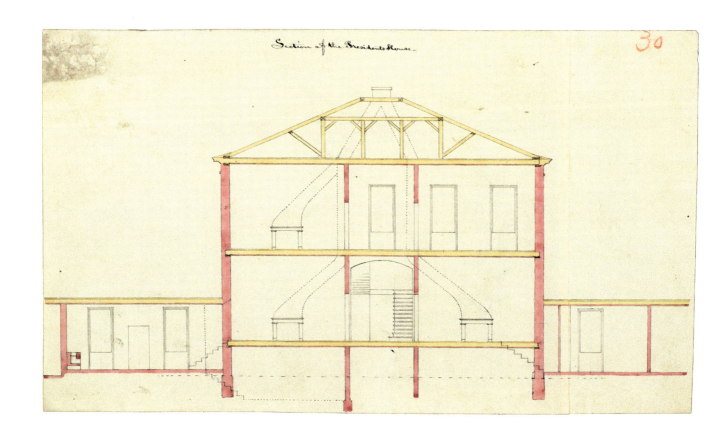

35 President's House
Section drawing

Pearson #30

Black ink and transparent watercolor over faint graphite and compass pinpricks with brown ink inscription; red crayon pencil numbering on cream wove paper.

Paper extended at right edge.

9 ½" x 16 ⅝"

SPECIAL COLLECTIONS, SCHAFFER LIBRARY, UNION COLLEGE

In this longitudinal section drawing, red indicates brick walls and yellow-brown indicates wood floors and roof structure. The dotted lines above the fireplaces show where the flues rise within the walls. There is an inconsistency between this drawing and the floor plans of the house, which show second-story rooms in the wings on the left and right sides of the building. It is possible that when Ramée made the section drawing, he decided there was not enough height in the colonnades to have a second floor here.

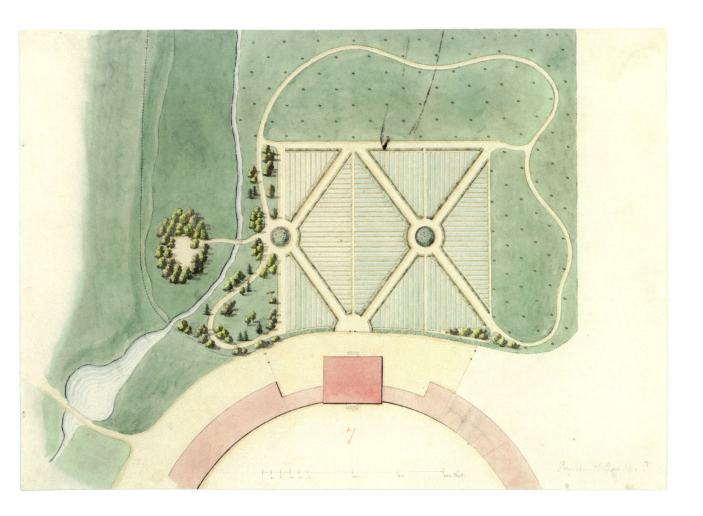

36 Plan of landscaping behind house with watercolor

Pearson #7

Black ink and transparent watercolor over faint graphite and compass pinpricks with brown ink inscription; red crayon pencil numbering on cream wove paper.

12 9/16" x 18 ¼"

SPECIAL COLLECTIONS, SCHAFFER LIBRARY, UNION COLLEGE

This sheet has no title, but it shows the President's House (in red), the semicircular colonnades attached to it (in pink), and the landscaping behind the house—the focus of this plan. It is an intriguing drawing in several respects. One question is whether Ramée intended it as a plan to be executed, or whether he was only experimenting here with various ideas. The latter possibility is suggested by the peculiarly asymmetrical nature of the landscape design, with most of the area used for a geometric pattern of planting beds (probably kitchen gardens), while the left-hand quarter of the pattern is replaced by completely irregular landscaping. It was typical of Ramée to combine formal and informal components in his landscape plans, but usually in discreet locations—not joined in the oddly hybrid manner seen here. If he was merely trying out different possible modes for the area behind the President's House, he apparently then chose the geometric pattern, for that is the design used in the most complete site plan of the campus (cat. 22). Supporting the opposite possibility, however, is the fact that the landscape is rendered with great care and detail, as Ramée did in his finished plans, not in experimental sketches. If he did think of this as a plan that might actually be executed, its daring eccentricity would be most unusual—perhaps unprecedented—in the architecture of this period.

Also notable in this drawing is the stream that runs through the informal landscaped area and widens into a small pond, to the left of the President's House. Presumably, this is a diversion of Hans Groot's Kill, done here in a different way from the diversion Ramée showed in his completed site plan (cat. 22). The cavalier manner in which he played with an impractical idea like this could be another indication that the drawing was experimental and fanciful, not seriously intended for execution.

THE GRAND DESIGN

COLONNADES

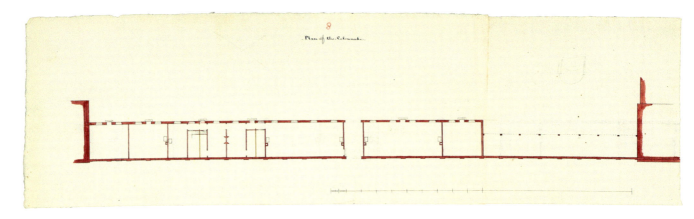

37 Plan of colonnade attached to South College

Pearson #8

Black ink and transparent watercolor over faint graphite and compass pinpricks with brown ink inscription and red crayon pencil numbering, on cream wove paper with "T G & CO" watermark.

8 ⅞" x 31 ⅜"

SPECIAL COLLECTIONS, SCHAFFER LIBRARY, UNION COLLEGE

This long sheet, like the following one, was produced by gluing together two strips cut from a sheet that had a floor plan of the Central Building (see cat. 17 and 18), so the reverse side of the newly-made sheet could be used. This was done when the Central Building project had been abandoned and Ramée was developing a new campus plan that included long arcaded structures. The architect, probably following President Nott's instructions, called these structures "colonnades" ("arcades" would have been a more accurate term), and the word has been used at Union College ever since.

In this plan, the northeast corner of South College is on the right side; on the left is the end wall of the building at the eastern end of the Colonnade. Using the scale at the bottom of the sheet, we see that the Colonnade shown here is about 360 feet long, with its enclosed parts twenty-five feet wide. The façade facing the central campus space (the wall at the bottom of the sheet) is divided into twenty-eight bays, or recessed sections of the wall, separated by piers. By contrast, each of the Colonnades that were actually constructed, in 1815, had only twelve recessed bays. The much longer Colonnades shown here are seen also in Ramée's most complete site plan (cat. 22).

The eight bays at the western end of the Colonnade are open on the back side, with only posts supporting the roof, and probably were intended to be stables. The rest of the Colonnade is divided into rooms that appear to be classrooms, which was in fact the main function served in the early years of the College by the Colonnades that were built. In Ramée's plan, access to these rooms is only from the back side of the Colonnade, while the constructed Colonnades also had doors opening onto the central campus space. Perhaps as a result of this matter of access, Ramée in this plan shows one of the bays as being open on both sides, thus serving as a passageway from the central campus space into the area behind.

Only two of the rooms in the Colonnade (two of the smaller rooms) are provided with fireplaces. Most of the rest of the spaces are shown with room-heating stoves.

38 Plan of colonnade attached to North College

Pearson #12

Black ink and transparent watercolor over faint graphite and compass pinpricks with brown ink inscription and red crayon pencil numbering, on cream wove paper with "T G & CO" watermark.

8 ½" x 31 ¼"

SPECIAL COLLECTIONS, SCHAFFER LIBRARY, UNION COLLEGE

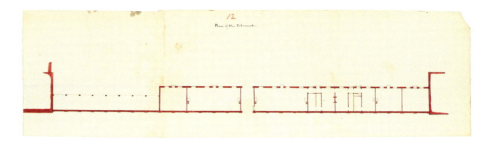

This plan is the same as that of the South Colonnade, but reversed. At the left is the southeast corner of North College.

JOSEPH RAMÉE

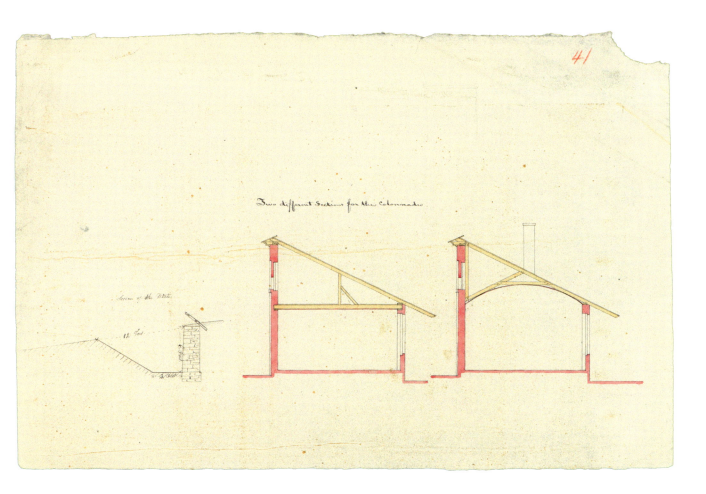

39 Section drawings for the colonnades

Pearson #41

Black ink and transparent watercolor over faint graphite and compass pinpricks with brown ink inscription; red crayon pencil numbering on cream wove paper.

11 ⅝" x 18"

SPECIAL COLLECTIONS, SCHAFFER LIBRARY, UNION COLLEGE

In this drawing, Ramée experimented with alternate ways of designing the interiors of the Colonnades. Red indicates brick walls and pavement, yellow-brown the wood structure of the ceilings and roofs. Probably the most unusual feature of the Colonnades is the use of the shed-roof form—a type of roof with only one slope, rather than the more common gable roof or hip roof. Ramée's motive for using the shed roof was apparently to give the Colonnades the appearance of thin planes, without visible roofs, when seen from the central campus space. As a result, there was less volume inside the Colonnades than a normal roof would have provided, and Ramée was faced with the question of whether a second floor could be accommodated. In the section drawing on the left, a small second-floor room is made possible by having a relatively low ceiling on the first floor, while the section drawing on the right provides a more commodious space below, with a vaulted ceiling, thereby sacrificing useful space above. When the Colonnades were actually constructed, at least some of their interior spaces did have two floors.

To the left of the section drawings is a small drafted sketch that seems unrelated to the Colonnades—a section through a stone retaining wall, in front of which the ground is graded to create a depressed area or ditch. The drawing is identified, in difficult-to-read handwriting, as "Secion of the Ditche." One might question whether this was even drawn by Ramée, but a similarly-shaped land form is seen in one of the marginal sketches in catalogue number 21, in a location that seems to be the ground that slopes westward from the Terrace Wall and North and South Colleges. This was apparently the ditch-like form that was commonly called a "Ha-ha," created for the purpose of keeping sheep or other animals within a grazing area, without having a wall or fence to impede the view of observers. It is something that would have interested Ramée, with his concern for how the Union College campus would appear to people approaching it from the west.

THE GRAND DESIGN 53

CORNICES

40 Cornice profiles for colonnades, President's House and "small colleges"

Pearson #25/26

Black ink and transparent watercolor over faint graphite and compass pinpricks with brown ink inscription; red crayon pencil numbering on cream wove paper.

22 ¼" x 18"

SPECIAL COLLECTIONS, SCHAFFER LIBRARY, UNION COLLEGE

This is the only sheet for which Pearson assigned two numbers, 25 and 26, for the two cornice-profile drawings on it. (Several of the other sheets also have more than one drawing, but Pearson may have given separate numbers to these two profiles because they belong to separate buildings.) The upper drawing, numbered 25, is labeled "Profile of the Cornich for the two Colonnades." The lower one, 26, is labeled "Profile of the Cornich for the President's House and small Colleges". The reference to "small Colleges" is intriguing. In Pearson's list, he describes drawing number 2 (one of the missing drawings) as "A plan ... in which Philosophical Hall and Geological Hall are called 'Small Colleges'." Philosophical and Geological Halls are the buildings at the ends of the colonnades that extend eastward from North and South Colleges. It is also possible, however, that Ramée and Nott used the term "small colleges" to refer to the two buildings in Ramée's design that are similar to North and South Colleges (but slightly smaller, having only one pavilion), toward the back of the campus, aligned with the rotunda, and connected by a semi-circular arcade to the President's House. Like North and South Colleges, these buildings were apparently intended as student dormitories, with faculty residences in the pavilions.

The handwriting that identifies these profiles may not be Ramée's. But next to the lower profile, in small writing in pencil, are the words, "M'on du Président et petit collège" ("President's House and small college"), surely written by Ramée himself. Some faint sketching, no doubt also by Ramée, can be seen in the margins of this sheet.

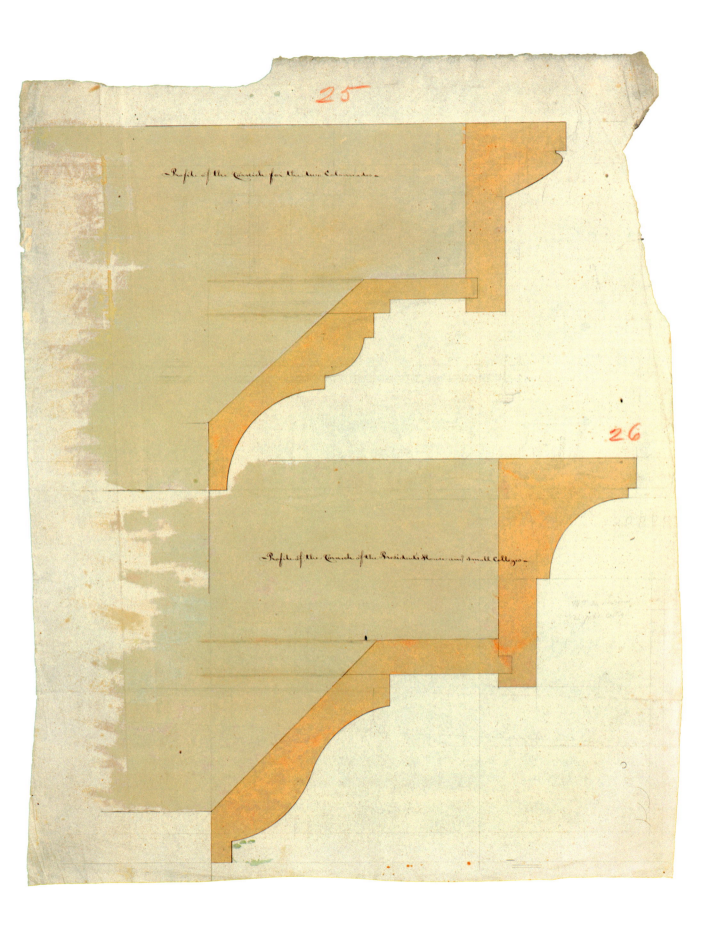

STEWARD'S HOUSE

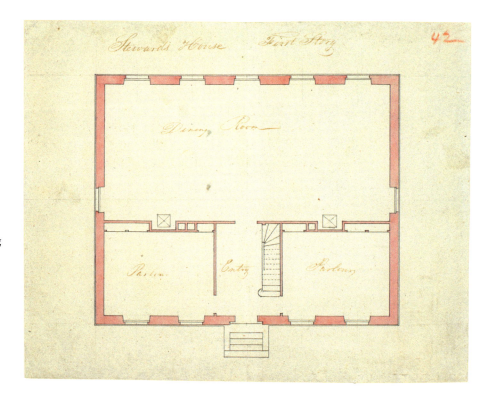

41 Stewards House
First story plan

Pearson #42

Black ink and transparent watercolor over faint graphite with brown ink inscription; red crayon pencil numbering on cream textured wove paper.

8 ½" x 11"

SPECIAL COLLECTIONS, SCHAFFER LIBRARY, UNION COLLEGE

The Steward's House was the college dining facility. Floor plans of the first story, second story, and basement of the building are among the surviving Ramée drawings; there was also an elevation drawing, which is now missing. These plans were presumably used for the two dining facilities that were constructed in 1814 and 1815 but no longer exist: South Hall, located where the current President's House stands, and North Hall, set back from the opposite end of the Terrace Wall. The two buildings are indicated on Ramée's site plans for the campus (such as cat. 22) and are shown in both the Klein engraving and the Givens painting.

The first floor has a large dining room, with two rooms called "Parlour" at the front of the building. There are no fireplaces in the house, except for one in the kitchen in the basement (perhaps used for cooking); most of the other spaces are shown with room-heating stoves, probably of the type designed by President Nott.

A fourth drawing of the Steward's House, now missing, is listed on Jonathan Pearson's inventory of the Ramée drawings: "36. Stewards House—front Elevation (North & So. Halls?)." It was not noted by Codman Hislop as one of the missing drawings when the portfolio was discovered in 1932, but there is no documentation of its existence in the following years and it was recorded as missing in 1984.

42 Stewards House
Basement plan

Pearson #37

Black ink and transparent watercolor over faint graphite brown ink inscription; red crayon pencil numbering on cream textured wove paper.

8 ½" x 10 ⅞"

SPECIAL COLLECTIONS, SCHAFFER LIBRARY, UNION COLLEGE

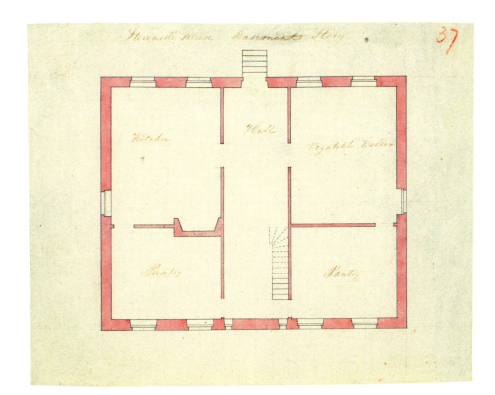

The central circulation hall in the basement leads to the kitchen, a "vegetable cellar," and two pantries.

43 Stewards House
Second story plan

Pearson #11

Black ink and transparent watercolor over faint graphite brown ink inscription; red crayon pencil numbering on cream textured wove paper.

9" x 10 ⅞"

SPECIAL COLLECTIONS, SCHAFFER LIBRARY, UNION COLLEGE

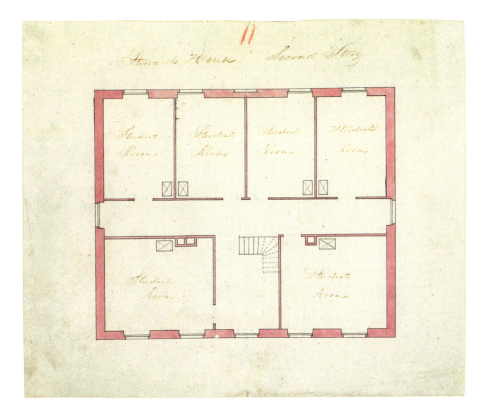

The plan of the second floor is shown as having six "Students" rooms, to supplement the dormitory facilities in North and South Colleges. Each room has a space-heating stove.

THE GRAND DESIGN 57

LECTURE HALL BUILDING

44 Lecture Hall Building

Plan, elevation and section drawings of amphitheater shaped building with two lecture halls

Pearson #44

Black ink and transparent watercolor over graphite with graphite inscription on textured cream wove paper.

19 ¼" x 13 ⅛"

SPECIAL COLLECTIONS, SCHAFFER LIBRARY, UNION COLLEGE

This sheet has a floor plan, elevation drawing, and two section drawings of an amphitheater-shaped building containing two semicircular lecture halls—the building connected by a free-standing wall to the corner of another structure. Each of the lecture halls in the building has two sloping tiers of benches in the curving end of the room, the upper tier supported on four columns. In the middle of the building, where the hemispheres abut, there is an opening between the two spaces where lecturers would stand, suggesting that one lecturer might be able to address both lecture halls at the same time. It is an unusual building, especially for an American college of this period, and it may have no precedent in earlier educational architecture in the United States. Its source seems to be amphitheatrical lecture halls in French schools of the period.

No building of this shape is seen on any of the site plans among the drawings found in 1932, but one does appear in the lithographed plan for Union College published in Ramée's *Parcs et jardins*, and the nearly identical drawing discovered in Paris in 1890 (cat. 3 and 4). In these plans, the building is located behind South College and South Colonnade. If Ramée had this location in mind when he did the drawing for the lecture-hall structure, the building to which it is connected by a free-standing wall would be South College.

The drawing is not included on Pearson's list of the Ramée drawings. It has the number 44 written on it, but Pearson's list ends with the number 43, and "44" appears not to be written in Pearson's hand. At the end of the list, someone (perhaps Hislop) later wrote, "44 – Small amphitheater or lecture hall …," implying that the drawing was in the portfolio discovered in 1932; but Hislop's article in the *Union Alumni Monthly*, describing the drawings in the portfolio, does not include this one. These facts might lead one to question whether the drawing was in fact the work of Ramée. But the characteristics of the drawing itself are fully consistent with his other drawings, and the fact that a similarly-shaped building is shown in the *Parcs et jardins* plan of the college also indicates that Ramée was its author—as does the French nature of the design itself. It is one of the most fascinating of his drawings for Union College.

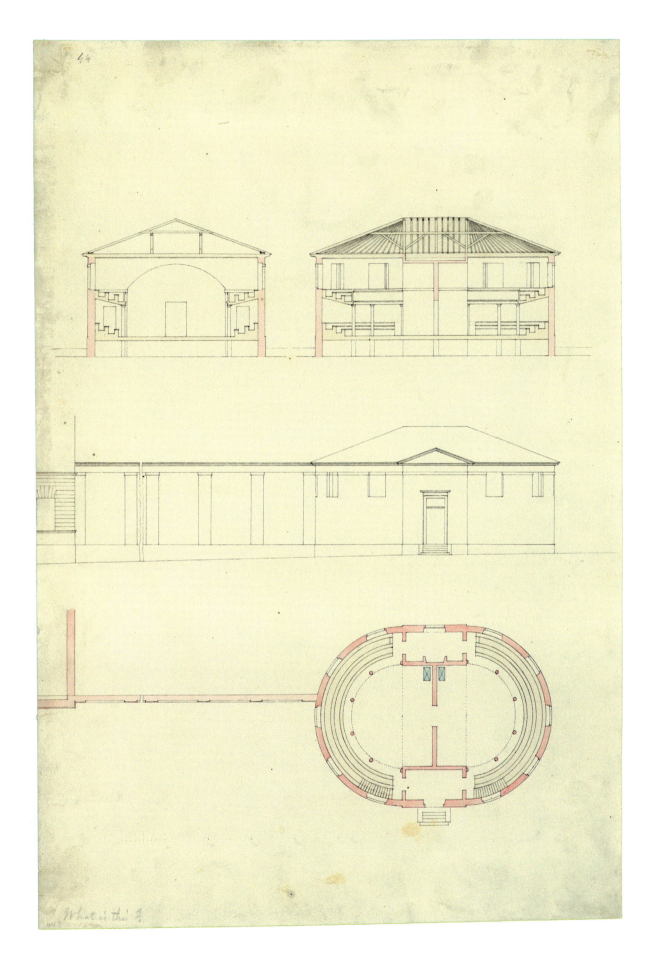

THE GRAND DESIGN

DORMITORY STRUCTURE

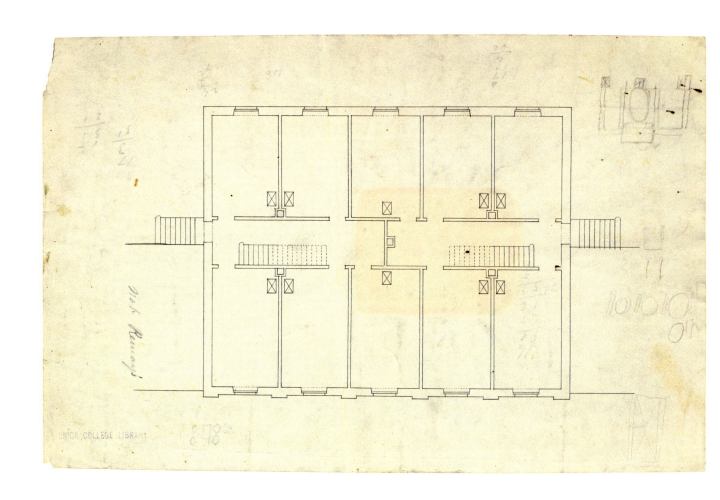

45 Dormitory Structure

Plan of unidentified small structure containing students' rooms

Pearson #27v (Verso of cat. 22)

Black ink over faint graphite and compass pinpricks with graphite inscription on cream wove paper.

19 ¼" x 13 ⅛"

SPECIAL COLLECTIONS, SCHAFFER LIBRARY, UNION COLLEGE

This drawing, which is on the back of the sheet bearing Ramée's watercolor site plan (cat. 22), is the first-floor plan of a multistory structure containing students' rooms—planned no doubt to supplement the dormitory space in North and South Colleges. At one side of the drawing is the penciled notation "not Remay's," probably written by Pearson (who spelled Ramée's name this way). It is unclear how Pearson, who was too young to have had firsthand experience of Ramée's design of the college, would have known who did the drawing; but in fact he was probably correct. The plan is not drafted as skillfully as were Ramée's drawings, and the sketches in the margins are amateurish, without the surety that even Ramée's most hastily sketched drawings have. Moreover, it is difficult to imagine that the architect would have put a drawing on the back of his fine watercolor site plan of the campus. Apparently someone else later drew this dormitory plan on the back of the sheet.

ACKNOWLEDGEMENTS

This exhibition and accompanying catalogue have truly been a collaborative effort. However, I owe most of my thanks to Paul Turner, author of the catalogue, for his scholarly essay and meticulous catalogue entries. He would like to extend his thanks to Wayne Somers, author of the *Encyclopedia of Union College History*, for his help with the project. I also want to thank Ellen Fladger, Head of Special Collections, Schaffer Library, and her assistant, Marlaine Deschamps, for retrieving the drawings repeatedly from storage when necessary. I want to thank Eric Seplowitz for creating digital images of every drawing reproduced here. Brigham Taylor helped with proofreading the manuscript. Rebecca Johnston, paper conservator from Williamstown Conservation Center, examined the drawings for media descriptions. Elizabeth Laub-Zick designed an extraordinarily elegant volume to showcase Joseph Ramée's work. My assistant, Sarah Mottalini, has been invaluable at every step of the process.

—Marie Costello, Interim Director of the Mandeville Gallery

ELIZABETH LAUB GRAPHIC DESIGN / PRINTED BY SNYDER PRINTERS

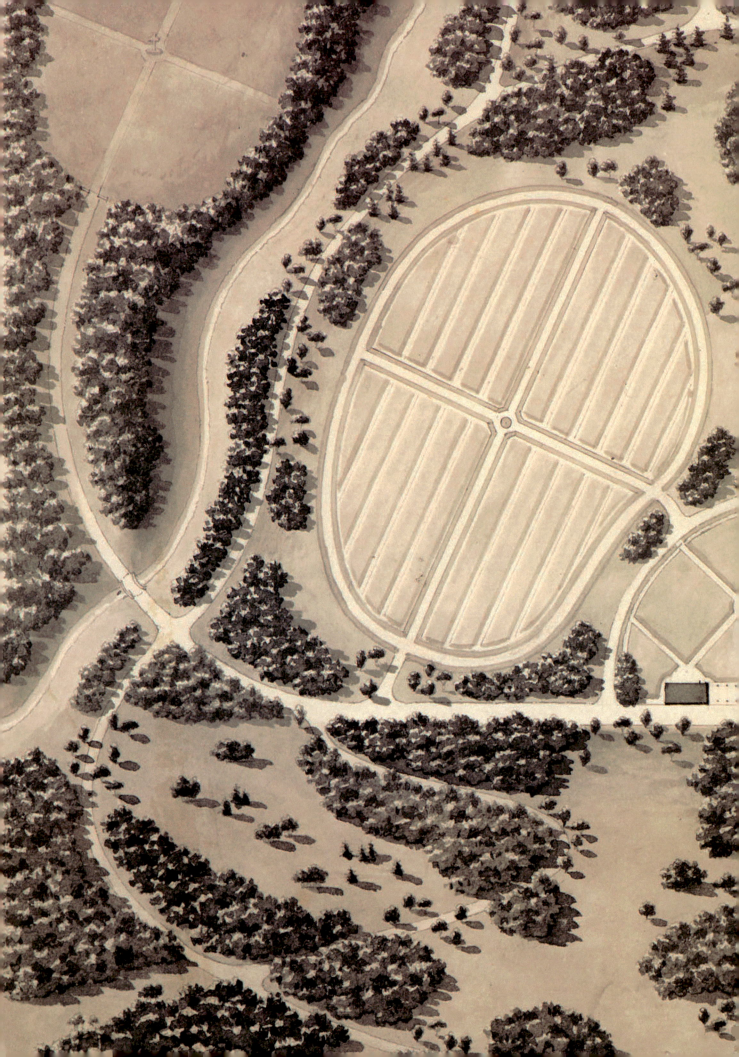